MANAGING CONTINGENT WORKERS

MANAGING CONTINGENT WORKERS

How to Reap the Benefits and Reduce the Risks

STANLEY NOLLEN
AND HELEN AXEL

amacom

American Management Association

New York • Atlanta • Boston • Chicago • Kansas City • San Francisco • Washington, D. C.
Brussels • Mexico City • Tokyo • Toronto

This book is available at a special
discount when ordered in bulk quantities.
For information, contact Special Sales Department,
AMACOM, a division of American Management Association,
135 West 50th Street, New York, NY 10020.

This publication is designed to provide accurate and authoritative
information in regard to the subject matter covered. It is sold with the
understanding that the publisher is not engaged in rendering legal,
accounting, or other professional service. If legal advice or other expert
assistance is required, the services of a competent professional person
should be sought.

Library of Congress Cataloging-in-Publication Data

Nollen, Stanley D.
    Managing contingent workers : how to reap the benefits and reduce
the risks / Stanley Nollen and Helen Axel.
        p.   cm.
    Includes bibliographical references and index.
    ISBN 0-8144-0242-9
    1. Temporary employees.   2. Personnel management.   3. Temporary
employment—Cost effectiveness.   4. Temporary employees—United
States—Case studies.   I. Axel, Helen.   II. Title.
    HF5549.5.T4N65   1995
    658.3'044—dc20   95-37870
                                                      CIP

Printing number

10   9   8   7   6   5   4   3   2   1

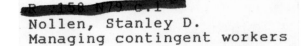

Contents

Figures

Tables

Acknowledgments

Our first acknowledgment is to Barney Olmsted and Suzanne Smith of New Ways to Work, who conceived and implemented the Equiflex Project that marked the beginning of the company research conducted for this book. We are grateful to Paul Rupert and Gil Gordon, who provided leadership for this project, and to the business managers who were members of the Equiflex Project and whose insights and experiences are found in the contents of this book. Financial support was obtained in part from the Alfred P. Sloan Foundation with assistance from Program Officer Hirsh Cohen and the Rosenberg Foundation and Program Officer Kirke Wilson.

We thank in particular the companies and managers who participated in our field research: Kelly Murphy, Marcia Van Skiver, and Tom Pierson of Hewlett-Packard; and Marcia Worthing, Ron Shane, Barbara Foster, and Josef Wolf of Avon Products. We are equally grateful to the other managers whose companies are not identified but who nevertheless provided valuable information and opinions.

Many other experts gave us assistance on particular aspects of the research, including Thomas Nardone of the U.S. Bureau of Labor Statistics and Bruce Steinberg of the National Association of Temporary and Staffing Services.

Preface

This book begins with an overall discussion of the different categories of contingent workers and their place in the business world. In subsequent chapters we review your strategy in using contingent workers so that your company can become a more informed and effective employer of these workers. You learn about ways to use and manage a blended workforce, how contingent workers fit into different work sites, and how their costs stack up against those of regular employees. Step-by-step information is provided about how to measure the costs and cost-effectiveness of your contingent workers. And you discover how you can avoid overreliance on contingent labor.

Information for this book is derived from the experiences of various companies, specifically case studies among five large corporations. The case studies examine contingent employment in selected operations of two financial services companies, two electronics manufacturing firms, and one consumer products company. Although these case examples offer detailed information about contingent jobs and workers, they are not representative of all contingent work, and the company-specific findings cannot be generalized. However, the case studies do provide insights into management practices and certain aspects of each are likely to be relevant to various employers.

Chapter 2 examines strategies for using contingent labor. We start with the business objectives served by a contingent workforce and continue with the ways in which contingent workers are used—how many are used, the types of jobs they do, and which staffing option to choose. We look at the problem of ''creeping contingency'' and show how contingent labor is affected by downsizing. We explain the core-ring model, and offer guidelines for managing a mixed workforce of both contingent and core employees.

Chapters 3, 4, and 5 are dedicated to the central question of achieving cost-effectiveness in the use of contingent labor. Chapter 3 lays out the factors that shape the cost-effectiveness result and shows how to determine cost-effectiveness in your work unit. Chapter 4 uses intensive case studies to report on the cost-effectiveness experiences of three companies. Chapter 5 brings together lessons learned from experience to improve the chances for cost-effective management of contingent labor.

Chapter 6 shifts the focus to the workers. It argues that equity and fairness issues need to be confronted and solved in order for companies to get the best from their use of contingent labor. Using two case studies, we focus on issues of workers and the relationship between contingent workers and core employees.

Chapter 7 takes up some of the legal considerations that have grown up around the increasing use of contingent workers, ranging from issues of de facto co-employment relationships to tax liabilities.

Chapter 8 is a summing up and looking ahead chapter. The emphasis is on communicating a practical set of management guidelines to assist in the cost-effective and equitable management of a contingent workforce in the future.

S.N.
H.A.

MANAGING
CONTINGENT
WORKERS

1

Familiar Issues, New Concerns

Since the mid-1980s, a growing volume of articles in the business press has attested to fundamental changes in the way companies structure their workforces. The relationship between employer and employee is being radically altered. The phrase *contingent employment*, referring to people whose work is contingent on a company's need for them, was first used by Audrey Freedman, then a labor economist at The Conference Board, during Congressional testimony in 1985. Before that time, little attention had been paid to the growing number of people who did not hold regular full-time jobs but who were more marginally attached to the workforce.

The awareness is much greater today. A speculation repeated in the business press is that as many as 50 percent of all workers will be contingent by the year 2000. Others take the core competency fashion to an extreme and argue for outsourcing everything except what you do better than anyone else. They predict that "virtual employment" will become the norm as companies form temporary alliances with a wide range of suppliers of products and services and contracting out becomes the usual practice. Still others observe that today's job insecurity has already made everyone in the labor force a disposable worker. In most major corporations, managers no longer speak about permanent employment for anyone; instead they advise "employability" for everyone.

In large measure, the current unsettled work environment accounts for the almost single-minded attention in business to cost control, leanness, and flexibility. A shrinking corporate core workforce is the most visible outcome of these efforts. One popular part of the strategy to trim down and shape up makes use of contingent workers. Evidence from available statistics and anecdotal information reveals that companies are using more of these workers more extensively and for more diverse assignments than ever before.

Employer Expectations and Concerns

The spreading use of contingent labor has blurred the boundaries between the jobs traditionally done by marginally attached workers and the jobs reserved for regular employees, and it raises questions about the management decisions behind these changes. There is growing concern, for example, that many decisions to shift to contingent labor may be based on assumptions about its advantages rather than arrived at through advance planning or economic analysis, and that overreliance on an externalized workforce may prove to be a costly "solution" for the employer.

Although contingent jobs satisfy the needs of some workers who want more flexible work patterns, employers may be the losers as they populate their workplaces with people who have little attachment to their jobs. And there are some contingent workers who do not want to be so unattached in the first place. At a time when *customer service* and *product quality* are the operative watchwords, companies can ill afford to have less committed workers delivering their products and services.

But few employers have taken stock of their actions. Companies that have downsized indiscriminately, for example, have found that simply eliminating large numbers of people from the payroll does not make the work vanish (and, by the way, does not reliably make the stock price go up for long). In many instances, companies have found themselves in the unexpected position of having to rehire regular employees or add temporary staff in order to satisfy customer demand and meet production deadlines. And in many industries, including service-sector businesses, where contingent jobs have always been prevalent, expanding their use into areas previously assigned to regular employees may, in the long run, cost the company dearly if core expertise is not retained in-house.

In these times of cost-consciousness, companies now more than ever need to ask themselves whether heavier reliance on contingent labor will produce the benefits they hope for. Professor Jeffrey Pfeffer of the Stanford University Graduate School of Business puts it this way in his book *Competitive Advantage Through People:*

> If competitive success is achieved through people—if the workforce is, indeed, an increasingly important source of competitive advantage—then it is important to build a workforce that has the ability to achieve competitive success and that cannot be readily duplicated by others. Somewhat ironically, the recent trend toward using temporary help, part-timers, and contract workers, particularly when such workers are used in core activities, flies in the face of the changing basis of competitive success.[1]

Companies need to increase flexibility and decrease costs. Will adding more just-in-time contingent workers accomplish these objectives? Is there a limit to how many contingent workers you use? How do they relate to the regular workforce? Do they work side-by-side with regular employees? What about the regular workforce? Can additional flexibility be obtained from it? Or is the lack of job security for regular workers creating unexpected resistance and rigidity that is exacerbated by emphasizing a two-tiered workforce? Flexibility to change quickly the number of workers and hours worked—numerical flexibility—may not be all that your company needs. Can flexibility in the skills people have and the jobs they do—functional flexibility—supplement numerical flexibility?

Contingent workers are often assumed to be cheaper than regular employees, but a cost analysis is seldom done. How cost-effective are your contingent workers? Have you assessed all the costs involved in shifting more work to an externalized workforce? Have you evaluated the kinds of jobs these workers should be doing? How much training is necessary to get contingent workers up to speed? Do contingent workers stay on the job long enough for you to recover the training investment?

Another set of issues centers on the management of contingent workers. Are your contingent workers managed directly by your supervisors, or do you have a representative from a staffing company on-site to deal with their problems? Do you use the contingent workforce as a screening device for recruiting new regular employees? Do you have different performance standards for contingent workers?

How do you compensate these workers? Does pay increase with per-formance or length of service? Are you adequately informed about the legal issues involved in your relationships with your external workforce?

Although these concerns may not all relate to your situation, it's likely that some of these questions have been raised by managers in your company. Contingent work may have many advantages for you, but a thoughtful analysis of how these workers are already used, and may be used in the future, should be actively explored.

Who Is a Contingent Worker? What Is Contingent Work?

The phrase *contingent employment* is not only finding a place in to-day's business vocabulary, it is also freely used by journalists and others as a catchall term for a variety of work arrangements that seem to have common features but are, in fact, quite different. At the same time, an entire vocabulary of alternative labels—such as interim, just-in-time, and supplemental—has also taken hold, further complicating efforts to make distinctions between the various forms of contingent labor.

According to the broadest concept, the contingent workforce would encompass all people whose jobs do not fit under the umbrella of regular full-time employment. This would mean that anyone who works a reduced schedule or anyone who doesn't work for someone else, however steady or secure those jobs might be, would fall into the category of contingent employment along with temporary work-ers and on-call part-timers. In some cases, even telecommuting and other off-site work could be viewed as nontraditional—and thus more tenuous—employment.

From a practical standpoint, such inclusiveness causes problems. The overbroad concept of contingent workers includes people who have freely chosen their reduced schedules or independent work status, as well as those who want regular full-time jobs but have to settle for something less, often part-time work. People who prefer or elect part-time employment can have a high level of attachment to their company, and people who choose self-employment can have a high degree of job security and stability. Vast differences in attach-ment of workers to employers, not to mention skill and pay, can be gathered under such a broad concept of contingent work. With such a range, the common features of contingency are obscured by the differences. In this book, the term *contingent labor* is used in a narrower context.

To define contingent labor in just a few words, we describe who contingent workers are and say what their work schedule is like:

> Contingent workers are people who have little or no attachment to the company at which they work. Whether they work, when they work, and how much they work depends on the company's need for them. They have neither an explicit nor implicit contract for continuing employment.

Contingent workers are "on-call" workers. Their work depends on—is contingent on—the work to be done, according to the company's call.

This simple definition conveys the idea and the spirit of contingent employment, and it describes the practice of using contingent labor in the abstract. But it does not tell us exactly who a contingent worker is. For this we need defining, concrete, and measurable characteristics. We propose three, in addition to the fourth overarching and subjective characteristic of "little or no attachment to the company." No one criterion by itself marks out a contingent worker, but taken together, these characteristics narrow the range of ambiguity. Note at the outset that contingency is not an indelible mark; a person can be a contingent worker now but not next year. It is a status that one can move into or out of, at least theoretically.

1. *Job insecurity.* Contingent workers usually have little or no job or employment security. They may or may not know when their current job or work assignment will end, and the company may or may not know, but neither worker nor company expects long service with the company. They may work a day or a year, but not a lifetime. Correspondingly, contingent workers usually change from one company's workplace to another's frequently. (While regular employees also have less and less job security these days, and in fact few people spend their entire career at one company, there is a mutual expectation between employer and employee of continuing service. Also, although some regular employees also change companies several times during their work life, these changes are often at their initiation and

done for career-enhancing reasons, unlike the company-instigated changes of contingent workers.)

2. *Irregular work time.* Contingent workers often have irregular work schedules. Both the total number of hours they work in a year and the days, weeks, or months when they work are unstable and dependent on management decisions rather than their own preferences.

3. *Lack of access to benefits.* Contingent workers usually do not have the access to benefits that regular employees in the same workplace do, or they may not actually receive them. Such benefits range from vacation leave to health insurance to pension benefits. Nor do contingent workers usually participate in the full range of other privileges and opportunities that are often available to regular employees, such as membership in company clubs, fitness centers, or eligibility for continuing education. Although benefits are not universally available even to regular employees, and some benefits surely could be made available to contingent workers, the fact that they usually are not creates a boundary between regular and contingent workers (see Chapters 2 and 6 for details and sources).

4. *Lack of attachment to the company.* This defining characteristic encompasses all the others, but it is scarcely measurable except in subjective ways. It is a sense, a feeling in both the worker and the manager. Contingent workers do not belong to the company as regular employees do; they are not expected to be as committed to the company's mission. They may be as fully committed to the work they do as regular employees are, especially among highly skilled professional and technical people. But they do not have the same ties to the company where they do the work.

The definition of contingent labor according to the criteria of attachment, job security, work schedule variability, and access to benefits is in accord with the views of U.S. Bureau of Labor Statistics researchers.[2]

Despite these defining characteristics, people do not go around companies with a label on their heads saying that they are contingent workers or regular employees. Instead, workers have a status such as part-time or full-time. If we are to really understand contingent labor in the terms of the labor market, we must relate it to these well-understood concepts.

Contingent workers are found among temporary workers, part-time workers, leased workers, independent short-term contract workers, and self-employed workers.

Temporary workers who are supplied from staffing companies have no attachment to the client company where they work. They have no job security at that company (although some temporaries are employees of a staffing company for several years), they move from one client company to another frequently, they have irregular work schedules (from one assignment to another, if not within one assignment), and they get no benefits from the client company. However, temporaries who are employees of one staffing company for long enough are probably eligible for some benefits. Agency temps are clearly contingent workers. (Three terms are used for the organizations that supply temporary workers: *agencies,* the traditional term; *staffing companies,* the new term preferred by the companies themselves; and *help supply services,* the term used in government statistics.)

What about temporary workers who are directly hired by the company where they work, perhaps as part of an in-house temporary labor pool? They differ from regular employees insofar as they move from one assignment to another, and usually their work schedule is irregular, at the company's discretion, and less than full-time. They may also feel less attachment to the company. But they are employees on the payroll, and may or may not have benefits. Most direct-hire temporaries would also be classified as contingent workers, but perhaps not all of them.

Part-time workers are often contingent workers but not always. Many people who work part-time by choice are regular employees just as much as full-time employees are regular employees. They have no less job security than full-timers, they have stable work schedules and annual salaries, long service with their company, and they typically get prorated benefits. They are not contingent workers, even though they may feel less attachment to the company if they have a primary interest outside the company that keeps them from working full-time. Other part-timers, who are paid hourly, denied benefits, and treated as on-call workers just like temporaries, are contingent workers.

Leased workers are different from temporaries supplied by staffing companies. Leased workers are employees of a company that takes on the operation of certain functions (e.g., administrative support) or staffs an entire office or factory on a contractual basis for a client company that in effect outsources these tasks. Often leased employees are former employees or independent contractors of the client company who have been transferred to the payroll of the leasing company. Leased employees may or may not lack attachment to the client company at which they work, and their employment continuity with that company or the leasing company may vary widely. They do not change work sites so frequently as temporaries, and they do have stable and predictable work schedules, with benefits paid by the leasing firm. Leased employees are considered contingent workers by the client company, although they have an employment relationship with the leasing company.

Independent contractors are contingent workers. They have a more predictable work schedule than temporaries do—they know when their job ends, by contract. And because they are not employees of any company or agency, they have in principle more choice about their work.

Self-employed workers include the independent contractors just described. These people may be retirees, sometimes employees who have opted for early retirement. Or they may be employees who were forced out of the company during a restructuring or downsizing; they are hired back not as employees but as independent contractors. Other times, these contract workers are an alternative to temporaries from agencies. Of course, many self-employed people are not contingent workers. They are independent businesspeople such as doctors and lawyers. (See Table 1-1, in which these points are summarized.)

Issues discussed in this book do not cover so-called permanent part-time employees, some of whom are former full-time workers who have reduced schedules for personal reasons and are expected to return to full-time work at some later date. Since these workers are generally carried on the employer's regular payroll and receive benefits prorated according to hours worked, they are really part of a company's regular workforce.

Our analysis also does not deal specifically with contingency as it relates to jobs of well-paid consultants and other self-employed professionals who can enjoy their independent status because they have highly marketable skills and thus little concern about their continued employability. While these people may look like contingent workers according to our definition, they raise few of the management problems encountered among nonprofessional workers or pro-

Table 1-1. Who is a contingent worker?

Staffing Option	Defining Criteria				Result: Contingent Worker?
	Attachment to Company*	Job Security	Work Schedule	Benefits	
Temporary workers, from agencies	no	no	irregular	none from company; some from agency	yes
Temporary workers, direct hires	no for some, yes for some	no for some, yes for some	irregular for some, stable for others	yes for some, no for some	yes for most
Leased workers	no for some, yes for some	no for some, yes for some	stable for most	none from company; yes from leaser	yes for some, no for some
Short-term contract workers	no	no	stable for most	no	yes
Part-time employees	no for some, yes for some	no for some, yes for some	irregular for some, stable for others	prorated for some, none for others	yes for some, no for some
Regular full-time employees	yes	yes (to the extent that security exists at all)	stable	yes	no

*Attachment to company for temporary and leased workers refers to the client company where the work is done.

fessionals who are former employees of their clients and are dependent on them for continued contracts.

Recent Trends in the Contingent Workforce: What the Numbers Show

How many contingent workers are there? How fast is the contingent workforce growing? These are simple questions, but there are no good answers yet. No one knows for certain what the numbers are, although the popular belief is that the numbers are big and growing fast. A decent guess at the upper and lower bounds is that in 1993 contingent workers accounted for 20 to 25 percent of the U.S. workforce, and that these numbers are increasing, but not explosively.

We do not know exactly how many contingent workers there are because of the imprecise definition of contingent labor, and because of these workers' relative lack of attachment to their workplace. Thus, the number of contingent workers has not been measured in nation-wide statistical surveys. Luckily, this fact gap is being filled by U.S. Bureau of Labor Statistics tabulations of new data collected especially for this purpose. In the meantime, we try to approximate the number by using data that are in hand. The best we can do to estimate the size of the contingent workforce is to add up the number of people who fall in the categories that contain contingent workers—part-timers, temporaries, leased workers, and independent contractors.

Early estimates of the size of the contingent workforce were done by Audrey Freedman in 1985 and by Richard Belous of the National Planning Association in 1989. Belous said that between 25 and 30 percent of the entire U.S. workforce in 1988 was contingent workers.[3] Belous built up this figure from part-time employees, temporary workers, self-employed people, and employment in the business services industry (the latter was used only for the higher 30 percent figure). If Belous's methods are used and the figures updated, the contingent workforce amounted to 27 to 31 percent of the entire workforce in 1993. These numbers appear too high; we reestimate them below.

Part-Time Employment

Part-time employment in total accounted for 19.2 percent of all employment in 1993. Voluntary part-timers—people who choose to work part-time—were 13.8 percent of all employment, and involuntary part-timers—people who could find only part-time work or whose work hours were cut back because of slack work—were 5.3 percent of all employment (the latter figure includes people who usually work full-time).[4] Many people who are part-timers involuntarily surely are contingent workers (their work schedule depends on the amount of work to be done), but many people who are part-timers by choice are regular core employees. In fact, more than half of all part-timers have a regular daytime work schedule, and only 17 percent have an irregular employer-determined work schedule. A generous guess is that at most 80 percent of all part-time employees are contingent workers, putting their share of the workforce at a maximum of roughly 14 percent (this estimate makes use of data that are mentioned in Chapters 2 and 6 on the occupations of part-timers and the benefits they receive, as well as the information above).

Temporary Workers

Employment by temporary help supply services accounted for 1.4 percent of all employment in 1993 and 1.65 percent in 1994, according to the National Association of Temporary and Staffing Services. However, the often-quoted statistic that Manpower, Inc. is now the nation's largest employer is often misleading. The claim is based on the total annual throughput of employees at Manpower over a year's time rather than on a count of active employees at any one point in time. Because turnover at staffing companies is obviously quite high, the former figure dramatically overstates the latter. The percentages stated above include the "permanent" employees who manage the services as well as the people who receive temporary assignments. However, they still do not accurately reflect the number of temporary workers because many temporaries come not from an agency but are hired directly by the companies that use them. These direct-hire temporaries outnumber agency temporaries, probably by a wide margin. According to speculation from fragments of data about these people (one source is Katherine Abraham, "Flexible Staffing Arrangements and Employers' Short-Term Adjustment Strategies," in Robert A. Hart (ed.), *Employment, Unemployment, and Labor Utilization.* Boston: Unwin Hyman, 1988), direct-hire temporaries may have accounted for 2 to 4 percent of the workforce in 1985. A generous estimate for the share of all temporary workers in the workforce in 1993 is 4 to 6 percent. Of course, some of these temporaries work part-time hours (about 40 percent, according to Belous) and are therefore double counted.

There is no separate measure at all for the number of independent contract workers; most are included among either part-time or self-employed workers and some are probably invisible in the statistics.

If we add part-time contingent employees and all temporary workers (and eliminate double counting), we get at most 18 percent of the workforce that is contingent labor. If we further add some self-employed people and people who work in the business services industry who are neither part-time nor temporary (such as full-time short-term contract workers and some leased employees), we might arrive at our estimate that contingent workers make up about 20 to 25 percent of the workforce. (See Sidebar 1-1 for some international comparisons for contingent labor.)

(Text continues on page 15.)

▾▾▾

SIDEBAR 1-1

International Comparisons: How Big Is the Contingent Workforce in Other Countries?

Is the United States different from other countries in the use of contingent workers? Is the U.S. growth record for contingent workers different? The answers are yes—vast differences exist across countries in the use and growth of part-time employment and temporary workers. In some countries, only 5 percent of the workforce is part-time or temporary, and in other countries, the figure is more than 30 percent. Some countries have doubled their reliance on part-time employment while others have decreased it.

The United States is right in the middle among industrialized countries in its usage of part-time employment, yet near the bottom in growth of usage. The countries with the highest usage of part-time employment are the Netherlands (33 percent of total employment in 1990), where both government and labor unions have encouraged it as a way to reduce unemployment, and the Scandinavian countries (23 to 27 percent of total employment).[5] The countries that least use part-time employment are the Mediterranean European countries—Greece, Italy, Spain, and Portugal—with 5 to 6 percent of the workforce in part-time jobs (see Figure 1-1). The Netherlands, Great Britain, and France have shown the fastest growth in part-time employment.

The United States appears to be on the low end internationally in its usage of temporary workers, although the lack of U.S. data on direct-hire temporary workers makes strict comparisons impossible. If temporary employment in the United States is roughly 4 to 6 percent of all employment ($1\frac{1}{2}$ percent from agencies and a guess of 2 to 4 percent as direct-hires), the, according to 1991 statistics, it is similar to what is found in Great Britain and represents the lowest figure among industrialized countries. The country with the highest use of temporaries (including temporaries from agencies and workers on fixed short-term contracts) is Spain, which has the lowest use of part-timers. Conversely, the country with the highest use of part-timers—the Netherlands—is among the bottom in the use of temporaries (see Figure 1-2). To some extent, part-timers and temporary workers can be substitutes. The countries with increases in temporary employment were Spain and France, and, it appears, the United States.

▲▲▲

Figure 1-1. Part-time employment across countries, 1990.

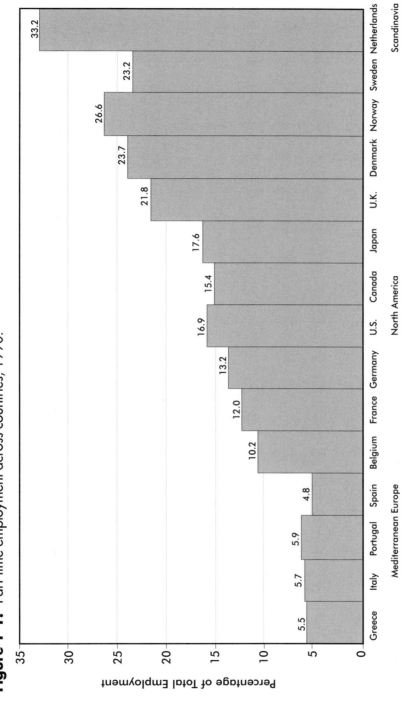

Source: OECD Employment Outlook, 1991.

Figure 1-2. Temporary employment across countries, 1991.

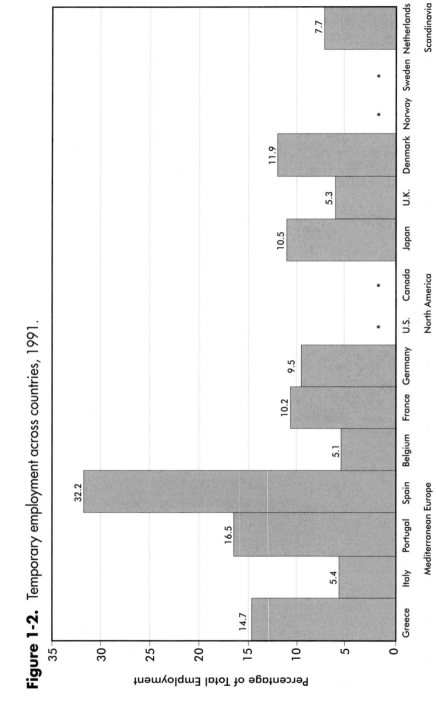

Note: Data include temporaries from agencies and workers employed directly on short-term contracts.
* = not available
Source: OECD Employment Outlook, 1993.

How Fast Is the Contingent Workforce Growing?

Rapid growth in the contingent workforce is taken as fact by most people. It is only partly true. It is true for temporary workers, where growth has been explosive in the 1980s and 1990s to date. The share of temporary workers from help supply services in total employment tripled from the recession year of 1982 up to 1994, and increased six times from the early 1970s to 1994 (keep in mind that the big increases are from a small base). The use of temporary workers tends to go down in recession years as companies shed labor, and increase a great deal during strong growth years (see Figure 1-3).

Rapid growth is not the case for part-time employment. Voluntary part-time employment has not changed as a percentage of all employment since 1970. The only growth has come from boosts in involuntary part-time employment during recessions (unlike temporary workers, where the pattern is reversed). Workers are forced into part-time work during economic hard times, as in 1974, 1982, and 1991, when they can't find full-time jobs (see Figures 1-4 and 1-5).

If the assertion of Belous in 1988 that the contingent workforce as a whole was growing fast is revisited in 1993, five years later, we see a slowdown. Using his measures, we see growth in temporary employment (still from a small base) and in business services employment (used only in his upper boundary estimate of the size of the contingent workforce). However, because temporary services are included in business services, there is some double counting. We see no real growth in part-time or self-employment (see Figure 1-6).

Behind the Growth

No one who has observed the business environment during the last 15 years can fail to recognize the vast changes that have taken place in the workplace during this period. Nor can anyone be unaware of the circumstances underlying these changes: the reality of a global economy and a global marketplace and resulting significant shifts in business resources and the emergence of new competitors; ongoing technological breakthroughs that continue to change the way work is performed; and a workforce no longer homogeneous and no longer

(Text continues on page 20.)

Figure 1-3. Trends in temporary help employment in the help supply industry.

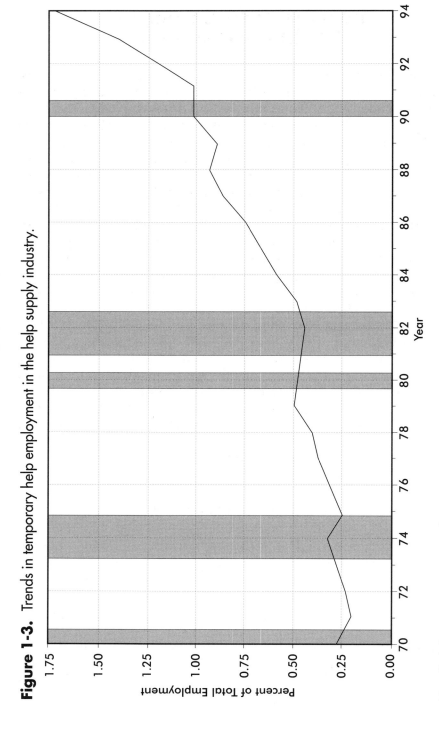

Note: Shaded areas are recession periods.
Source: National Association of Temporary and Staffing Services (data from U.S. Bureau of Labor Statistics and NATS surveys).

Figure 1-4. Trends in part-time employment.

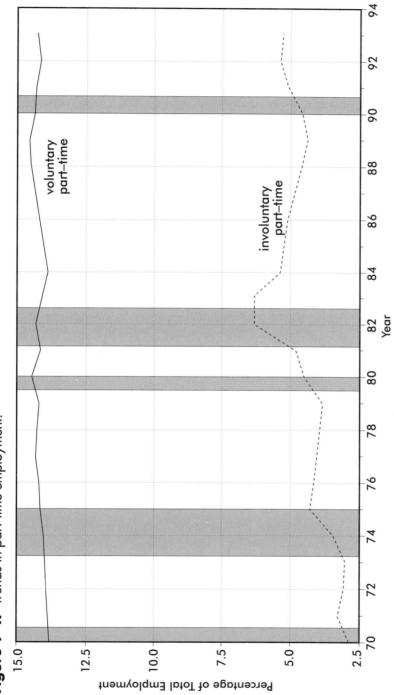

voluntary part-time

involuntary part-time

Percentage of Total Employment

Year

Note: Shaded areas represent recession periods. Data for 1994 are available but not directly comparable with data for 1993 and earlier years.
Source: Employment and Earnings, various issues, U.S. Bureau of Labor Statistics.

Figure 1-5. Change in involuntary part-time employment over time.

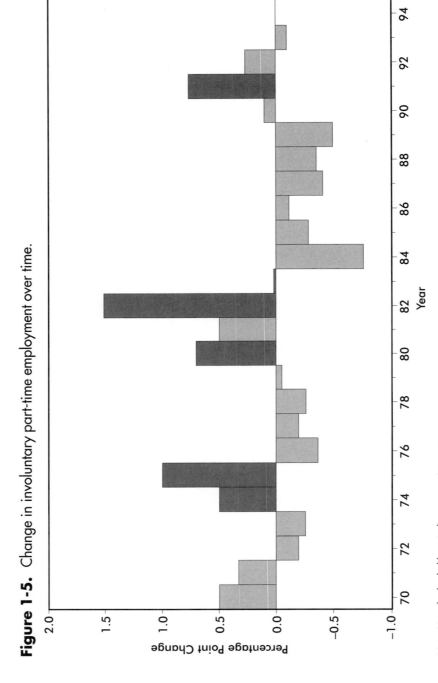

Note: Heavily shaded bars indicate recession years.
Source: *Employment and Earnings*, U.S. Bureau of Labor Statistics.

Figure 1-6. Trends in the contingent workforce.

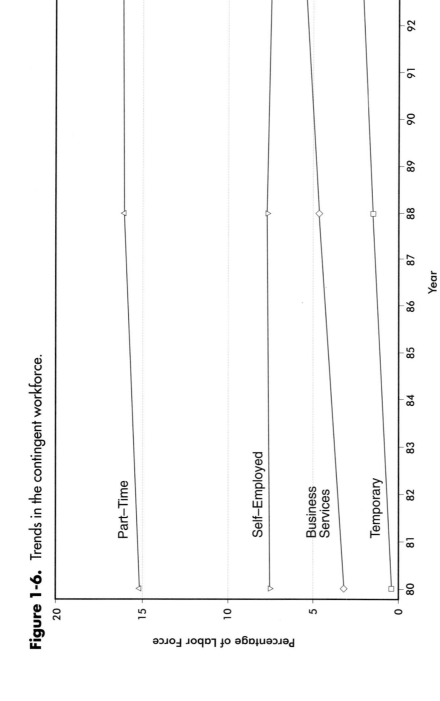

Source: Belous (1989) and *Employment and Earnings,* U.S. Bureau of Labor Statistics, 1994.

dependent on paternalistic employers. Companies caught up in this turmoil find their efforts to restructure and position themselves for survival and growth to be an ongoing struggle. Their actions, as well as structural changes in the economy and the workforce, have contributed to the growing number of contingent workers.

Restructuring and Downsizing—
Fewer Core Employees

The restructuring fever, which began in the early 1980s at the same time as a serious recession, continues as a prevalent business strategy today, with downsizing as its most visible consequence. During the 1990s, according to annual surveys by the American Management Association (AMA), almost half of all companies have experienced workforce reductions, and many have been repeat downsizers (see Chapter 2 for more details and a reference to the AMA surveys).

Amoco, which eliminated 8,500 jobs in 1992, announced plans in mid-1994 to drop another 3,800 employees, reducing its 4,200-person corporate staff to about 400 within the year, as reported in the *New York Times*, July 22, 1994. The end result, according to the company, is an estimated workforce reduction of about 25 percent overall—with no assurance that the trimming will stop there. This is but one example. Anyone can easily find other stories like this by merely turning the pages of a business newspaper for a few days.

Then, too, the repeat process often drags on. When, in mid-1993, IBM's new top management announced another round of cutbacks, CEO Louis Gerstner expressed the hope that the company was "getting to the end of this adjustment process" (quoted in the *New York Times*, July 28, 1993). At the time, the company had already shed more than 150,000 jobs since its peak employment years in the mid-1980s. But achieving its goal to cut another 35,000 employees by the end of 1994 turned out to be a much slower process than Gerstner envisioned. Seven months into the year, IBM still had another 20,000 jobs to eliminate.

Although fewer companies report future downsizing intentions than have already downsized, AMA surveys show that such plans are consistently underestimated and often subject to revision. As one of many examples, Scott Paper Company announced in January 1994 its intention to cut 25 percent of the workforce within the next two to three years. By August, an upward revision of that number and a faster timetable indicated that one-third of the workforce, including 70 percent of its headquarters staff, would be dismissed by the end of the year (reported in the *New York Times,* January 27 and August 4, 1994).

Not only do companies revise previously announced plans, but also a majority of major corporations expect periodic downsizing to be a necessary activity for some time into the future as well, according to a Conference Board report (see Chapter 2 for more information and a reference).

The apparent unending pace of corporate restructurings and downsizings is all in the name of organizational leanness and flexibility. Jobs and workers must be eliminated, companies believe, so that they can operate more efficiently and respond more quickly to changes in market conditions. The logic is that a smaller workforce with fewer layers of management will speed decision making and trim overhead costs.

Although companies intend to function within the bounds of a slimmer core staff, many now find themselves relying more heavily on contingent workers—not only to take on short-term or temporary assignments, but also to replace talent lost in downsizing. To some extent, we are seeing the growth of contingent labor as a result of companies' miscalculations and mistakes. In these cases, unintended use of contingent labor makes cost cutting and productivity improvement goals harder to achieve.

In other cases, the move to contingent work is a deliberate strategy. A division of McDonnell Douglas, for example, aims to have a workforce composed of 10 percent contingent workers by 1996, with the expectation of savings from using just-in-time labor and avoiding benefits costs.[6]

Global Competition

Global competition is the lingo of the 1980s and 1990s—and for good reason. The United States imported less than 10 percent of its goods and services until 1977. Then the international trade deficit ballooned and caught politicians' attention in the early 1980s. Now imports, and exports too, are much more important to the economy. Investment abroad by U.S. companies and investment in the United States by foreign companies have increased even faster than trade in this time period. Barriers to trade and investment have been coming down. The

North American Free Trade Agreement was implemented in 1994 and the Uruguay Round of the General Agreement on Tariffs and Trade was concluded in the same year. Global competition is a reality like never before. And it affects contingent labor.

Two of the major consequences of global competition that grip many companies are intensified pressures to cut costs, and more rapid and more severe fluctuations in their need for labor. Imports compete with your product, or they are components of your product (or both); they force you to reduce your prices and your costs, or they threaten labor that was hired domestically. In either case, there is a new stimulus to shift to contingent labor, or to rely on offshore operations.

It happens to foreign firms as well as U.S. firms. A dramatic example occurred in Japan, a most unlikely place, in 1994 when money-losing Japan Airlines began advertising for 100 flight attendants who would be short-term contract workers paid by the hour and shed and rehired as passenger traffic demanded. In the meantime, regular full-time cabin attendants would be cut from 6,000 to 4,600 over four years, as reported in the *Financial Times*, 13 and 14, August 1994. Goodbye to lifetime employment; hello to contingent employment.

Investments abroad present opportunities to produce here or there, and some companies switch back and forth depending on changes in costs and markets. Until it sold its personal computer business to AST in 1993, Tandy made computers either in its Texas plant or its Taiwan plant. Labor forces have to be numerically flexible, and that introduces contingent labor.

Growth in the Service Economy

The upturn in contingent jobs coincides with the surge in employment in service industries, a sector where part-time and temporary jobs have historically been abundant. In 1992, the service sector had 27 percent of all employment in the U.S. economy; 20 years earlier, it had just 17 percent. Similarly, in 1994, 58 percent of total employment was in traditional white-collar jobs in administration, sales, and services, where both part-time and temporary employees are concentrated. Twenty years ago, the figure was 48 percent.

Within the service industries, as in other industries, expansion in contingent employment situations reflects the new employer mindset. According to economist Chris Tilly, a "low-wage, low-skill, high-turnover labor market, already apparent in corporate downsizing, has been widely adopted."[7]

One of the features of the service sector that links it to contingent employment is the fact that many services cannot be produced for inventory and stored for future delivery or use; they must be produced to order, on demand. This means that the workforce must be sufficiently flexible to grow and contract along with the fluctuations in the customers' demand for the service. It also means that traditional hours of work must be extended to meet customer requirements—hence the large number of part-time jobs often filled by contingents.

A new development in services is that the long-awaited gain in productivity expected from technological advance, mainly in computing, has been finally showing up. The resulting tendencies in the workforce in the short run are to reduce employment, or at least not to add staff (witness the so-called jobless recovery that showed only a 2 percent gain in total employment over the 1992–1993 two-year economic expansion), and to change the content of jobs to be done. Both tendencies stimulate contingent employment.

More Workforce Diversity

The growth in contingent employment is also linked to increased diversity within the workforce—more people who move in and out of the labor force, or who prefer part-time or temporary jobs because of competing demands on their time, different stages in the life cycle, or different family circumstances. The legitimizing of work-family and diversity issues within major workplaces over the last decade or so has undoubtedly made it possible for more employees with family or other personal obligations or interests to take advantage of alternative work arrangements within the core. It may also have encouraged more participation in the external workforce as well. Both the increased availability and variety of work arrangements and the changed demographics of the workforce are likely to stimulate each other.

One aspect of workforce diversity, age, has become less prevalent in recent years. Downsizing has had a leveling effect on the age distribution of the labor force, with the elimination of many older employees from corporate payrolls. Some of these 50-plus workers have joined the contingent workforce as temporary workers, consultants, or independent contractors, sometimes for their former employers.

A New Employer-Employee Contract

Upheaval in the workplace has dissolved the once-close bonds between employer and employee. Corporations are no longer willing to take on employees for their entire careers because they cannot be certain what business operations or jobs will be needed years into the future. Several years ago, for example, Xerox estimated that 25 percent of its jobs were unanticipated.[8] As a result of these uncertainties, companies have revised the terminology they use in discussions with employees about their future job opportunities. They now refer to *career management* rather than *career development,* and *employment security* rather than *job security.* Intel goes a step further by avoiding the use of the word "career" altogether, because it implies an upward progression. Intel's human resources vice president, who is quoted in a *Fortune* article of June 13, 1994, tells employees, "You own your own employability. You are responsible."

For their part, many employees are just as unlikely to commit themselves to a single employer because they foresee career growth as a multiple-company experience. Frequent disruptions from downsizing have also taken their toll on employee morale and loyalty. Both the survivors who have witnessed the turnover and the victims themselves are acutely aware of the precarious circumstances in today's work environment.

With both parties shying away from long-term commitments, the ties between them have been—perhaps irreversibly—loosened. The tendency for both companies and individuals is to expect and accept more fluid work relationships and less permanent forms of employment.

Endnotes

1. Jeffrey Pfeffer, *Competitive Advantage Through People* (Boston: Harvard Business School Press, 1994), p. 21.
2. Anne E. Polivka and Thomas Nardone, "On the Definition of Contingent Work," *Monthly Labor Review,* December 1989.
3. Richard Belous, *The Contingent Economy* (Washington, D.C.: National Planning Association, 1989).

4. These data and those that follow come from U.S. government statistics and are found in unpublished tabulations and a paper by Thomas Nardone, "Contingent Workers: Characteristics and Trends," 1993.

5. These data and those that follow are from two reports by the Paris-based Organization for Economic Cooperation and Development: "Non-Standard Forms of Employment," *Employment Outlook,* July 1991; and "Temporary Work," *Employment Outlook,* July 1993.

6. Shari Caudron, "Contingent Work Force Spurs HR Planning," *Personnel Journal,* July 1994, p. 54.

7. Chris Tilly, "Continuing Growth of Part-Time Employment," *Monthly Labor Review,* March 1991, p. 14.

8. Helen Dennis and Helen Axel, *Encouraging Employee Self-Management in Financial and Career Planning,* The Conference Board Report No. 976, p. 27.

2

Fitting Contingent Workers Into Your Workforce

Companies need flexibility. They need ways to rapidly increase and decrease the labor hours they employ as their need for labor changes. Powerful forces outside companies drive the flexibility need (see Chapter 1). Rapid and often unpredictable change, and relentless pressure to cut costs, force companies to increase workforce flexibility, and a favored way to get it is from contingent labor.

Once we realize the need for flexibility and the potential of contingent labor to meet that need, we run into questions about how to use contingent labor. These questions are in the forefront of management practice today, as illustrated by recent articles in the business press:[1]

> Tomorrow's organization certainly must turn a significant part of its work over to a contingent workforce that can grow and shrink and reshape itself as its situation demands. But note that even the most creative work design begs the question of how unready most organizations are to manage this workforce of temps, part-timers, consultants, and contract workers effectively.

> HR professionals will have to learn how to staff and manage the contingency workforce to the benefit of the com-

pany and all its various employees . . . (including) determining which employees should form the core work-force and what positions should be more fluid. Whether your company benefits from the advantages of a flexible workforce, or suffers from its inherent problems, will depend largely on the way contingent workers are managed.

In this chapter, we offer strategies for managing contingent workers. We look at how companies use them in practice and the specific business purposes they serve. We address the key management questions of which staffing option or type of contingent worker should be used and how to structure a mixed workforce of core and contingent workers.

How Companies Use Contingent Workers

The ways in which companies use contingent workers are varied, much more so now than in the past. Temporary workers don't just fill in for secretaries on vacation, and part-timers aren't just store clerks. Temporaries are also interim managers. The cover of a *Fortune* magazine showed a 49-year-old temporary executive who had run four companies in the last seven years. Companies are also hiring chief financial officers, marketing executives, and human resources professionals to work on an interim basis, and "lawyer-temps" have found their way into major U.S. law firms. Part-timers are also professionals, though the numbers in these jobs are still relatively small. (A statistical summary of the occupations of temporary workers and part-time employees is reported in Sidebar 2-1.) To illustrate how some companies are using contingent workers, we offer several concrete examples in the section that follows.

▲▼

SIDEBAR 2-1

Jobs for Contingent Workers—The National Picture

Nationwide, the jobs that contingent workers do are not at all representative of the whole range of jobs in the economy. Both part-time and temporary workers are concentrated in a few types of jobs, mainly at the lower end of the skill and wage spectrum. For example, among all part-time employees, 70 percent have sales, clerical, or service jobs. In fact, nearly half of all the people employed in retail sales jobs are part-timers, and more than one-third of all the people in service jobs are part-timers. Jobs in which part-timers are especially underrepresented are managerial positions and craft occupations workers. However, there are substantial numbers of professionals who are part-timers—15 percent of them as of 1992 (see Figure 2-1).

Temporary workers supplied from staffing companies are also clustered in just a few types of jobs. Close to one-half of these temporary workers were in a clerical or administrative job in 1985, but only one out of 12 agency temporaries was a manager or professional. The concentration of agency temporaries in these occupations is equally skewed. In 1985, 1.8 percent of all people in administrative jobs was an agency temporary, while only 0.3 percent of all managers and professionals was a temporary (see Figure 2-2). (These data are quite old, but they are the latest government statistics available. More recent occupational data are available from the National Association of Temporary and Staffing Services, but these data are reported in terms of payroll dollars, not numbers of people.)

▰▰

Data Entry in the Backrooms of Commercial Banks

Commercial banks use contingent workers in their backroom operations to enter data from checks and other paper documents into computer files for processing. Some banks use temporaries supplied from agencies; others hire hourly-paid part-time employees onto their payrolls. The backroom operations in two banks that we studied—Company A and Company B—have roughly 100 to 200 people in each backroom work unit. The offices are filled with keyboards and paper-handling machinery, and the employees work well into the night to process the previous day's bank branch business. Since the volume of data to be entered fluctuates enormously from day to day and week to week, the banks add and subtract labor hours every day to match the amount of work to be done. At Company A an average of one-quarter to one-third of the backroom workforce is made up of contin-

(Text continues on page 32.)

Figure 2-1. Occupations of part-time employees, 1992.

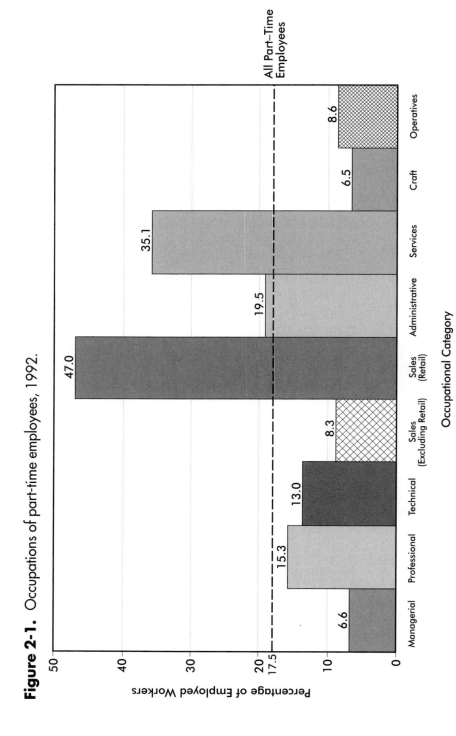

Source: U.S. Bureau of Labor Statistics, unpublished data.

Figure 2-2. Occupations of agency temporary workers, 1985.

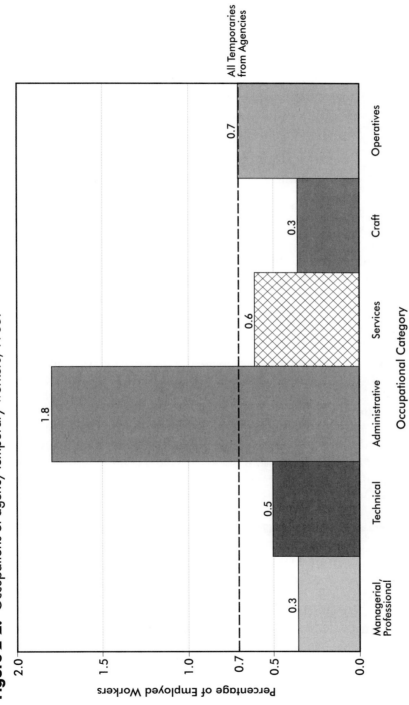

Note: Data refer to employees of help supply (agency) services only.
Source: U.S. Bureau of Labor Statistics, unpublished data.

gent workers, and at Company B the numbers of contingents run to half or more of all the people on the job. Regular core employees also do the same data entry jobs as contingent workers in both banks, but the contingent workers are concentrated in the lowest job grades. (See Table 2-1 for a summary of how contingent labor is used in these and a few other companies.)

Assembly of Components in Electronics Factories

Companies that make high-technology electronics products such as computers, laser printers, instruments, and automatic control systems use contingent workers in their factory assembly work. The companies that we studied—Company C and Hewlett-Packard—rely mainly on temporary workers supplied from staffing companies. Both companies want to protect their regular core workers from layoffs during business downturns and from losing their jobs when a product is phased out or a work unit is closed. Both companies face some unevenness in customer demand over the year and need to change the amount of labor on the job during that time period.

Company C uses quite large numbers of contingent workers— one-quarter to one-third of the total workforce at one factory location, or about 225 people. Hewlett-Packard's U.S. workforce is about 7 percent contingent labor overall, but in some small units that have a total of only 40 to 50 people, the figure could go temporarily as high as 50 percent. In both companies, core and contingent workers do some of the same jobs. At Company C, temporaries at one location work in teams with core employees but necessarily are concentrated in the more entry-level types of jobs. At Hewlett-Packard, temporaries frequently are used in clusters concentrated in specific functions and locations with more separation from core employees.

Picking and Packing in Consumer Products Distribution

The business of many consumer products companies is seasonal, especially so for a company we studied—Avon Products—which manufactures cosmetics as a main line of business and sells these products through its thousands of home-based representatives. Avon uses contingent workers in its manufacturing and distribution facilities to enable it to meet the peak fourth-quarter demand for its products without excessive use of overtime during the peak times or layoffs during the slack times. Avon's contingent workers are employees on the payroll who are on-call; they work full days part of the year, when needed.

Many of the jobs the on-call employees do are the same as the jobs that regular employees do: picking items from stock and packing them into boxes to make up the unique orders from customers, shipping the orders, operating the equipment to manufacture some of the items, or processing the paperwork for incoming orders. However, contingent workers are concentrated in just one low job grade, as in the bank operations described previously. (See Figure 2-3 for the job grades of contingent and core workers in these companies.) In a single location that has 700 to 1,000 people, perhaps 120 to 280 will be contingent workers.

Why Companies Use Contingent Workers

Companies need flexibility in how much labor they hire, and they need to control labor costs at the lowest possible levels. Contingent labor can meet both of these needs. Exactly how does it do so? And are there other business purposes that are served by a contingent workforce? We answer these questions with the reasons that companies themselves give for using contingent workers.[2]

Match the Workforce to the Workload

As is evident from the examples mentioned, work doesn't always come in eight-hour chunks five days a week. As demand for your company's products or services fluctuates, your need for labor also fluctuates. Contingent labor lets you make a better match between the amount of labor hours you pay for and the amount of work to be done. This is true for the two banks and Avon (as just described).

Hiring part-timers to meet peak demand periods and then letting them go is not a new idea for U.S. employers. We have always had part-time bank tellers and part-time store clerks. Temporary employment, also not new, is nevertheless becoming more widespread. Manufacturers using contingent labor are able to rely on less inventory and concentrate on immediate demand. In service industries, contingent workers help extend customer hours or fill in to meet periods of high demand.

(Text continues on page 37.)

Table 2-1. How contingent workers are used in seven companies.

Variable	Company A	Company B	Company C
Type of job and work unit	Data entry operators in bank backroom proof center	Data entry operators in bank backroom lockbox	Assembly of electronics components
Staffing option	Hourly part-time employees on the payroll	Temporaries from agencies	Temporaries from agencies
Number of contingent workers	Quarter to third of work unit; about 30–40 people average	Half or more of work unit; about 60 people average	Quarter to third of location; about 225 people average
Time on the job	Supervisor wants long term; actually about $1\,^1/_2$ years average	No company policy; actually about 7 months average	Limit of 1 year; actually about 7 months average
Reason for use	Match labor input to daily fluctuations in workload	Match labor input to monthly fluctuations in workload	Protect core workers from layoff; save costs; match uneven contract deadlines
Relation to core workforce	Same jobs done by both, but most part-timers in lowest job grades; no movement to core	Same jobs done by both, but temporaries concentrated in night shift; some hiring into core	Same jobs done by both, but all temporaries at lowest grade; some hiring into core

Note: Programs described here illustrate one use of contingent workers in one location in each of the companies but do not necessarily characterize companywide practices.
Sources: Company documents and interviews with company managers.

Hewlett-Packard	Avon Products	AT&T	Ernst & Young
Assembly of electronics components	Assembly, packing, shipping of consumer products	Clerical support for corporate headquarters units	Business support services for a main office
Temporaries from agencies	On-call part-year employees on the payroll	In-house temporary pool employees on the payroll	Outsourced from Tascor
<1% to >50% of work units, 5%–15% average, about 100 people	Quarter to third of location; about 250 people	Usually <10% in a work unit; about 300 people total	Quarter to third of work unit; 30–45 people
Limit of 2 years	Long term desired by company; actually 3 to 3$^1/_2$ years	9-month initial commitment, renewable	Depends on Tascor employee turnover, assignments
Protect core workers when work units are closed; staff new product start-up; match staffing with volatile or seasonal businesses	Match labor input to seasonal fluctuations in workload	Achieve staffing flexibility; avoid increasing regular workforce; curb growth of nonunion temporaries from agencies	Concentrate on core business; reduce cost
Same jobs done by both; contingents not intended to be source for core hiring	Same jobs done by both but more on-call workers in lower job grades; majority of contingents hired into core	In-house temporaries may apply for regular jobs after 9 months	No relationship to core workers; different jobs, no movement into core

Figure 2-3. Job grades of contingent and regular workers.

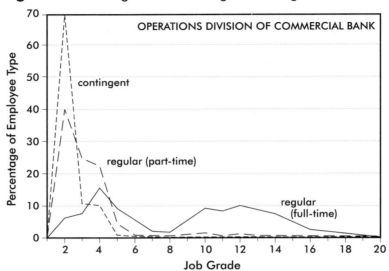

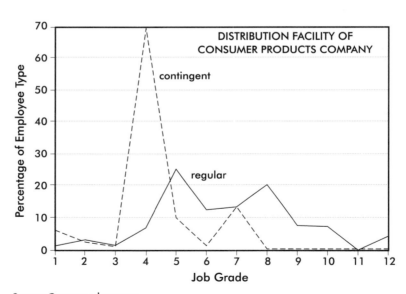

Source: Company documents.

Even in Japan, the land of lifetime employment, this reason to move to "just-in-time" labor is gaining adherents, as reported in the *Financial Times*, August 13, 1994:

> . . . The country's airlines . . . plan to hire new flight atten-
> dants on short-term contracts at sharply lower wage
> levels. . . . they aim to hire Japanese, largely for domestic
> routes, who would be paid by the hour and could not ex-
> pect to earn more than a third of the salary paid to their
> colleagues. . . . The contract staff who, although described
> as part-timers, would usually work a full week, could be
> shed and rehired as traffic demands.

However, the Japanese government temporarily stopped Japan Airlines from putting its plan into effect, saying that the plan would create two classes of employees who might not work together in sufficient harmony to be able to deal with an in-flight emergency. A month later the government relented.

Hiring "on-call" employees whose hours can be changed daily, or temporary workers who come when needed and go when not needed, solves the operational problem of getting the fluctuating volume of work done. And it saves money by not paying people who are idle when the workload goes down temporarily.

You can also use contingent labor in some cases as a substitute for overtime and layoff, the traditional methods of adjusting the number of labor hours hired. Overtime is expensive because wage payments per hour go way up. Layoffs are distasteful, also cost the company something, and don't work well for rapid adjustments.

Reduce Labor Costs

Contingent labor may be able to reduce your labor costs if these workers are paid less in wages and benefits than regular employees. (Caution: There are other employment costs above and beyond wages and benefits. As the discussion in Chapter 3 indicates, the cost-effectiveness of contingent labor is not a given. It depends on the nature of the job and other workplace conditions.) Time Inc. gives us an example, reported in *The Wall Street Journal*, March 11, 1993:

> Lou Capozzola worked 10 years at *Sports Illustrated* . . . as a
> lighting specialist. . . . In February 1990 he was called into

his boss's office and informed that his job was being eliminated, but that he could continue as an independent contractor. His base pay would be about halved to $20,000. His
overtime pay would be cut by as much as two-thirds. And
he could forget about his $20,000-a-year benefit
package. . . . Peter Costiglio, vice president for communica-
tions for Time Inc., says, "We looked at the job and our
needs and felt we could do it more cost-effectively on a
contractual basis."

Independent contractors, like Mr. Capozzola became, are contingent workers. If they accept less pay and no benefits while they do
the same job, the company cuts labor costs. Similarly, if temporary
workers and hourly part-time employees work for smaller wages and
fewer benefits but do the same work as regular employees, the company may also be able to cut labor costs. (Or so it seems; whether this
is really true in practice is examined in Chapter 3.)

In a March 1993 speech prepared for an investment conference,
the chairman of Rockwell International Corporation observed:

In our Space Systems Division . . . 8.7 percent of our salaried population is "alternative payroll" . . . by that I mean
flex force (temporary employees, retirees, and others), contracted services, or part-time. The annual per-person savings in overhead are almost $14,000 for contracted services,
$18,000 for part-timers, and more than $20,000 for flex
force, so figuring 8.7 percent of a salaried workforce of
more than 6,300, annual savings would run between $7 mil-
lion and $11 million or more, depending on the mix—and
that's just in one division.

Buffer Regular Employees From Job Loss

The approach of using contingent workers as a buffer against job loss
for regular employees was used formally by Control Data Corporation as far back as the late 1970s. In 1984, John Atkinson of Sussex
University in Britain wrote about a "core-ring" model.[3] Regular employees, both full-time and part-time, are in the core. The rings of the
model consist of contingent workers: temporary workers, hourly
part-time workers, independent short-term contractors, and others

(see Figure 2-4 later in this chapter). During recessionary periods, the people in the rings are most at risk, allowing some measure of employment security for those in the core.

The idea to create a buffer of contingent workers around regular employees as protection against layoffs in bad times gained popularity after the severe recession of 1981–1982 and was reinforced by the downturn of 1985–1986 in the previously high-growth computer industry. For some companies, layoffs cost too much in ill will and lost talent. Now these companies consciously keep their regular core workforce at a minimum level and add a buffer of contingent workers to absorb the shocks of business downturns.

Advertisements by Olsten Staffing Services that have appeared in major business magazines sell the idea like this:

> Upturns, downturns, recessions, depressions, sudden recoveries, and slumps. . . . It's the nature of business. When the economy goes, so do people. But layoffs cost money. And morale. Not the best way to adapt to a changing business environment. Olsten has the solution: flexibility. With the Olsten Flexible Workforce, the ability to respond effectively to economic trends is built into the structure of your company. During slower periods, maintain a core staff of full-time workers. Then when production increases and needs change, Olsten supplies you with appropriately skilled temporary workers.

Although most workers in the outer rings have very tenuous relationships with their employers, there are exceptions. At NCR's Engineering and Manufacturing plant in Atlanta, for example, a small core production workforce is supplemented by a group of on-call employees who are contracted to work at least 12 hours a week in four-hour stints that are determined by the individual workers. They also benefit from extensive training offered by the company, according to *Industry Week*, March 16, 1992.

Ease Management Tasks

If your workers are not your regular employees, you avoid many administrative tasks. Although contingent workers who are part-timers or on-call people are often employees on your payroll, temporaries from staffing companies, leased employees, and independent contractors are not. For these contingent workers, you don't need all the paperwork required for regular employees, nor do you need to provide the personnel services that core workers enjoy. Both ways, you can save money (see Chapter 3 for details).

The situation at B&G Glass Company illustrates the point. B&G Glass Co. is a small company in Livonia, Michigan, that began leasing employees in March 1990. The leasing company provided workers and, according to a story in *Nation's Business* in June 1991, "assumed responsibility for the bulk of B&G's personnel paperwork, which had been handled by the company's controller, Glenn Hoskins. . . . Hoskins finds employee leasing to be a valuable time saver. He says leasing 'has taken away a lot of headaches and made life easier for me so I can concentrate on the company's finances.' " However, there is a sequel to this story: In April 1994 B&G Glass stopped the leasing arrangement after the leasing company increased its charges. (Externalizing management responsibilities apparently also has its price.)

Like other temporary help firms, Manpower Inc. provides some clients with on-site management of its temporary employees who work exclusively for that client. One such client, Banc One, has a Manpower coordinator working in its Milwaukee offices to oversee the management of its pool of temporary workers. Recruiting, orientation, and training are handled by the coordinator, who is also the point person for all other human resources issues for these workers, as reported in *Training*, March 1991.

Making Intelligent Choices About a Contingent Workforce

To manage a contingent workforce in your company, you have to decide what staffing option is best—do you go for temporary workers, part-timers, short-term contractors, or something else? You also need to consider how many contingent workers you want in a work unit and throughout the company. There are questions about the jobs contingent workers will do and what strategies can be followed in designing a core-contingent workforce.

Strategy Before Structure

The starting point toward getting answers is the same one that you use in designing any business or employment practice. In plain words, you ask: What are we trying to do? What is our objective? In consulting terminology, it is putting strategy before structure.

Ask first what business purpose is served by contingent workers. For example, suppose the most important need you have is an operational need to rapidly add and subtract workers because of peaks and valleys in demand. Then the number of contingent workers you need is determined by the size of the workload fluctuations.

Or suppose that your most pressing need is to cut labor costs by cutting wage and benefit payments. Then you are likely to go for the largest number of contingent workers you can, consistent with good work unit performance—and that depends on how the work is done, how plentiful the supply of contingent workers is in your labor market, and whether they have the skills you need. Other factors may also have to be considered, however (see Chapter 3 on cost-effectiveness).

Or suppose that your primary objective is to increase the employment security of regular employees. Then the number of contingent workers you need depends on predictions of swings in employment levels in your facility over years of boom and bust. The employment structure most appropriate for you is probably the core-ring model, with an inner core of stable employment surrounded by rings of contingent workers of different types. If you ask company managers about the core-ring model, many will not know what it is. Yet many companies structure and operate a workforce according to the core-ring model. The model especially applies if the business purpose served by contingent labor is to buffer regular employees from job loss. (See Sidebar 2-2 for a description of the core-ring model.)

▼▼▼

SIDEBAR 2-2

The Core-Ring Model

The core-ring model provides a way to visualize the relationships between contingent workers and regular employees. In this model, the company's workforce consists of a core of regular employees, and rings of different types of contingent workers around the core from which the company obtains flexibility in the amount of labor used (see Figure 2-4).

Figure 2-4. Core-ring model.

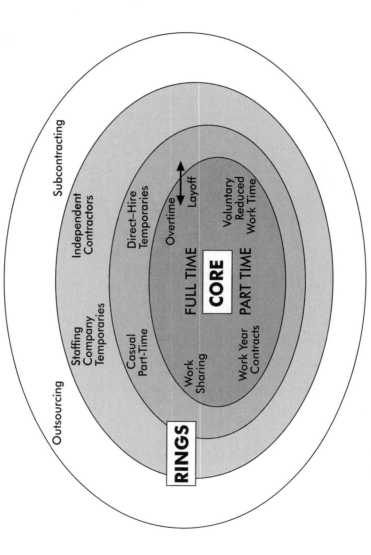

Source: Modified from John Atkinson, "Manpower Strategies for Flexible Organizations," *Personnel Management*, August 1984.

The makeup of the core and rings is as follows:

• *Core:* Full-time and part-time employees with regular or alternative work schedules and access to benefits, and with open-ended length of service expectations.

The traditional methods of adding and subtracting labor hours—overtime and layoff—are still used and shown in Figure 2-4 at the boundary of the core. Other methods of obtaining flexibility from the core, such as work sharing, are discussed in the next section of this chapter.

• *First Ring:* The ring that is closest to the core consists of contingent workers who are employees of the company and on the payroll: casual part-timers and direct-hire or in-house temporary workers. Their hours of work are changed or the jobs they do are changed by managers at will, but they can stay on with the company.

• *Second Ring:* The second ring out from the core consists of external contingent workers: temporaries from help supply services, leased workers, and independent short-term contractors. They are not employees of the company at which they work. They usually work a fixed schedule of full-time hours when they work, but they come and go as needed.

• *Third Ring:* The third ring out from the core consists of outsourced or subcontracted work done by employees (or contingent workers) of another company, frequently off-site. The people in the third ring are not necessarily present at the company that receives their output, but they are nevertheless a major source of workforce flexibility.

▬▬

If strategy is not in place first, how many contingent workers you have and where you use them will be correct only by accident. Without strategy, you are likely to end up with more contingent workers than you really want, doing work that they really shouldn't be doing. Downsized companies often find themselves in this predicament when large numbers of employees are terminated without controls in place to protect vital jobs and prevent a massive talent drain. Seeking an immediate solution, such companies then bring back former employees and temporaries to fill in the gaps and often assign them critical work that should not be relegated to outsiders.

Without strategy, the number of contingent workers tends to spread and grow—we call it "creeping contingents." In most companies it is easier to spend money to buy a service, including bringing in a contingent worker, than it is to create a position for a regular employee. For most managers, it is easier just to keep a contingent worker on the job than it is to restructure the work and employment optimally. That is how we get "permanent temporaries." Neither creeping contingents nor permanent temporaries belong in the intelligent manager's tool kit of employment practices. Both are undesirable defaults.

The Larger Business Context

To use contingent workers in the best way, you have to be conscious of linkages running from larger company strategies or campaigns down to patterns of use of contingent workers. Perhaps the most important trends today are downsizing and restructuring.

The Move Toward Downsizing

A company that downsizes—and by now that includes most companies—is likely to feel an impact on contingent labor, accidentally if not deliberately. Downsizing, which reduces employment in the company by eliminating excess labor, shrinks the core workforce. But it also might expand the contingent workforce and produce a de facto core-ring structure.

Company experience with how downsizing affects contingent labor can be inferred from survey data. A Harris survey done for The Conference Board in 1991 among companies that had downsized showed that about 10 percent of the companies "allowed many workers to work part time" as a downsizing action.[4] These part-timers may be either contingent workers or regular core employees. The same survey said that 37 percent of the companies listed "increased use of temporary workers and consultants" as a consequence of downsizing.

This rather high figure points out one of the ironies of downsizing. Many times it goes too far, leaving behind a case of "corporate anorexia." The use of temporary workers and consultants increases because the company loses the wrong people or loses too many people. Then the company has to bring in temporaries or bring back the same people whom it sent away—as contingent workers—in order to get the work done. An across-the-board cut of thousands of people is a very indiscriminant action.

The lesson from experience is this: Chances are that usage of contingent workers will not be right in a downsizing company—too many will be used and they will be used in the wrong places—unless a clear strategy is in place first, and the downsizing itself is done thoughtfully. (See Sidebar 2-3 for a brief status report on downsizing.)

(Text continues on page 48.)

▼▼

SIDEBAR 2-3

Downsizing and Restructuring: A Brief Status Report[5]

Downsizing

Downsizing means that employment is reduced. It may be across-the-board cuts, or it may be selective, surgical cuts. It may be the closing of an entire plant or the elimination of an entire function. In any case, the end result is intended to be the same: fewer employees.

Downsizing is not the same as a traditional layoff. Layoffs occur when business turns down and work is slack, and in most cases they are intended to be temporary. Laid-off workers expect to be recalled when business recovers, even if that is several months or even a year off. In contrast, downsized employees expect to be gone for good.

Downsizing started with this country's severe recession in 1982. Massive layoffs occurred then, but long after that recession ended, and in good times as well as bad, cutbacks in employment have turned into an apparently permanent way of corporate life. Downsizing has become an accepted and often recurring practice in U.S. companies. According to annual surveys by the American Management Association, close to half of all companies had shed workers in the years the surveys were conducted, and two-thirds of the companies that cut back in any given year did so again a year later.[6] Among Fortune 1000 companies, 85 percent downsized their workforces in the five-year period from 1987–1991, according to reports in the business press.[7] In 1993 the number of job cuts reached an all-time record of 615,000.

Companies that downsize include companies that are profitable and growing; it is not just a feature of declining companies or those that are operating in the red. Downsizing will continue as the need for companies to restructure and reduce costs continues. In 1991, two-thirds of surveyed managers said their companies were likely to eliminate jobs in the next five years, and more than half said that periodic downsizing would be necessary in the future.[8]

Why Do Companies Downsize?

Two main economic reasons motivate some corporate downsizing actions. First, companies downsize because they need to cut costs, especially overhead labor costs. This is the classic "cut out the fat" reason. Many times these costs are too high because of previous management errors—hiring was not controlled in good times, forecasts of future needs for labor were wrong, marginal performers were kept on too long, or cost controls were too weak.

Second, companies need to eliminate surplus labor. They experience a presumed permanent dislocation in their industry; e.g., new import competition, government spending cuts, or movement of production offshore. Or they need to shift the mix of labor and capital in production toward less labor and more capital, perhaps because of wage increases.

Two sets of organizational reasons for downsizing also apply. First, companies restructure and reengineer. They focus on core competences, outsource some functions (not just components), and eliminate other work from inside the firm. They take out whole layers of management They strive for less bureaucracy, faster decision making, more entrepreneurial spirit, and smoother communication.

A second organizational reason for downsizing leads to growth in contingent labor. The company wants to protect its workforce from future job loss due to industry dislocations or business downturns. It creates a core-ring model for its workforce. The aim is to reduce the size of the core of regular employees and add rings of contingent workers around the core as buffers to protect the employment security of the core.

Some downsizing efforts are motivated by a belief that a decisive move on the part of the chief executive officer to cut large numbers of employees is a demonstration to the financial community that the company is serious about getting its house in order—and that an increase in the company's share price will follow, thus pleasing investors, and aiding the job prospects for the CEO as well.[9] This is the "Wall Street" reason for downsizing.

Does Downsizing Work?

By now we know that downsizing does not work in many, many instances. Downsizing often does not achieve the objectives that companies expect from it. Less than half the companies surveyed by the Wyatt Company in 1992 said they reduced costs enough— managers ended up replacing some of the people they had dismissed. Only one in three companies said profits increased as much as expected, and only 21 percent reported satisfactory improvements in shareholders' return on investment. More than half the restructured companies surveyed by the Society for Human Resource Management said that productivity stayed the same or deteriorated after cutbacks. In addition, stock prices did not show improvement relative to the market or to comparable firms in the downsizing company's industry after two years, in a majority of cases.

Perhaps these unimpressive financial results stem from employee relations problems that all but the most skillfully executed downsizing can cause. When companies downsize, employees tend to become less willing to be creative or take chances. Survivors become more cautious and conservative. They lose their adaptability to change. They tend to distrust management and become less loyal to the company. Their outlook for the future becomes more negative, not more positive. These conclusions are based on a by-now sizable body of survey data and interviews with managers (previously cited).

Restructuring and Reengineering

Restructuring might be thought of as the intelligent offspring of downsizing. It often accompanies downsizing and is frequently used to connote downsizing. However, in its purest sense, companies don't restructure for the primary purpose of reducing employment or reducing labor costs, unlike downsizing. Instead, companies restructure to improve their long-term competitiveness, only one aspect of which is employment level and labor cost.

Restructuring is quite a broad and general term that includes decisions to change the businesses the company is in, to change the company's strategy for competing in those businesses, and to change the way in which the company makes products and services. The latter especially means that the structure of the company's workforce is subject to change. A changed workforce structure might or might not mean less labor is hired (downsizing might or might not accompany restructuring), but it probably does mean that a shift is made toward less core employment and more contingent labor.

Reengineering is a more technical younger first cousin of restructuring, as its name suggests. It has grown in importance since introduced by consultants Michael Hammer and James Champy in their 1993 book, *Reengineering the Corporation.* Both restructuring and reengineering make use of the immensely popular notion of core competence, which dates from a 1990 *Harvard Business Review* article by C. K. Prahalad and Gary Hamel, "Core Competence of the Corporation." The application of the core competence principle is likely to result in outsourcing, including labor.

The newest contender in the stable of management trends, and a part of reengineering, is, for lack of an apt label, "work-not-jobs." The idea is to abandon the notion of employment in companies consisting of jobs as packages of defined tasks, and instead to embrace the idea of employment determined by work to be done. When reengineering, don't think in terms of cutting jobs and people to get competitive. Instead think in terms of getting critical work done (probably in projects) by changing configurations of people (probably operating in teams). And think in terms of contingent workers—consultants and contractors as well as temporaries from agencies—to fit into other less critical work situations.

▛▲▲▲▜

The Move Toward Restructuring and Reengineering

Restructuring and reengineering are two more corporate imperatives of the 1980s and 1990s. Like downsizing, they tend to make the use of contingent labor go up.

While restructuring and reengineering usually do not explicitly seek to reduce employment levels in companies, streamlining work processes lends itself to cutting out unnecessary people, and often does change the mix toward less core employment and more contingent labor (see Sidebar 2-3). When you apply the concept of core competences (which is a part of restructuring and reengineering), you focus on those things that you do better than competing companies, and you outsource other functions that you previously did in-house. Outsourcing involves using employees of another company to do work previously done in-house, whether on your premises or theirs. If on your premises, the supplier company's employees become your contingent workers.

Another organizational trend is to see employment in a company in terms of work rather than jobs. Under this view, you are prompted to think of contingent workers. The excerpt from the *Fortune* article mentioned near the beginning of this chapter argued for the "end of the job" and concludes by asking:

- Is work being done by the right people?
- Are the core tasks—requiring and protecting the special competencies of the organization—being done in-house, and are other tasks being given to vendors or subcontractors, temps or term hires, or to the customers themselves?

If your company expects to downsize or restructure, chances are that the number of contingent workers will grow, partly by accident and partly by design. If your company is foresighted, however, you are armed with a strategy for using these workers so that you can maximize intentional—and minimize accidental—growth of your contingent workforce.

Which Staffing Option?

With regard to contingent labor, there are several staffing options available, one or more of which can be chosen for any particular work setting (see also Chapter 1):

- Temporary workers from a staffing company such as Manpower or Kelly or Olsten or one of many smaller local firms.
- Leased workers from an employee leasing company; these arrangements typically include groups of workers who are at the company for longer time periods than temporary workers.
- Temporary workers who are direct hires and thus employees of the company, and perhaps part of an in-house temporary pool performing a variety of tasks.
- Part-time employees who are on the payroll, often paid by the hour, as distinguished from part-time employees who are in the regular core workforce and whose work schedules are not subject to rapid or short-notice fluctuation.
- Independent contractors who are self-employed and work for a defined short-term period or do a defined project; these people may be consultants or freelancers (but not employees of consulting firms), rehired retirees, or downsized people.

This list does not come close to exhausting the range of options available that give a company workforce flexibility. For example, working time can be adjusted up and down to match fluctuating demand for labor by using work sharing or voluntary reduced work time among regular full-time employees, and annual work year contracts can be negotiated with either full-time or part-time employees. However, these alternatives are scheduling (as contrasted with staffing) options for regular employees rather than for contingent workers.[10]

If you ask company experts which contingent staffing option to choose, the answer is almost certainly going to be "it depends." On what does it depend? We suggest four areas for you to consider: (1) The nature of the work you have to get done, (2) the characteristics of your local labor market, (3) your existing policies and procedures, and (4) your organization's culture. You also need to be aware of the legal issues surrounding the use of contingent workers (the major legal problem areas are outlined in Chapter 7).

What Kind of Work Needs to Be Done?

Some types of work are better done by temporaries, some by part-time employees, and some by independent contractors. We can show this best by example.

If the work requires quite a bit of job-specific training or if it requires quite a bit of knowledge about the company, then you probably want part-time employees or leased employees as your contingent workers rather than temporaries or independent contractors. The reason is that you expect part-timers and leased workers to stay with you longer than temps or contractors; they can acquire the specific knowledge they need to be productive. (One reason companies like to rehire retirees as contingent workers is that they have company knowledge).

If the work can be done with quite a bit of autonomy so that good performance depends mainly on individual initiative, then you probably want independent contractors as your contingent workers. These people are accustomed to coming into a work situation, doing the work, and leaving; they don't need much orientation or interaction with others. This is especially true if the work demands a high level of specialized technical expertise.

If the work is very short-term and project-based, or special and nonrecurring, then you probably want temporary workers from a staffing company or independent contractors as your contingent workers rather than part-time employees who usually are kept on your standard payroll. This is the classic situation that fits temporary employment. You could also use direct-hire temporaries, who would move from one assignment to another in the same company.

If there are rapid-cycle fluctuations in workload so that labor input needs to be adjusted within a calendar quarter, month, or week, then you probably look to temporaries or on-call part-timers as your contingent workers rather than leased employees or independent contractors. The reason is that you can change the number of labor hours you assign day by day with temps or casual part-timers and thus match workforce to workload more precisely.

What Does Your Local Labor Market Look Like?

Two broad characteristics of the labor market from which you get workers shape your choice among contingent staffing options. The first is the supply of contingent labor. How many people are there in the market who are willing to work at contingent jobs in your company? How good are these people? Do they have the skills you need? Do they have the work habits you require? How easy is it to recruit them? If the answers to the questions are favorable, then part-time employees, direct-hire temporaries, and independent contractors are all viable staffing options. You can find them, they do good work, and their wage rates will be reasonable. Otherwise, you might want to rely on a staffing company or leasing firm. Of course, local labor market conditions change from year to year, so favorable answers now might not be favorable in the future. Furthermore, local labor markets can differ radically from each other or the national labor picture, so you can't infer very much from experiences in other labor markets.

The second issue deals with how well staffing companies meet your needs. The answer will differ across local labor markets. Most of the temporary service industry consists of local firms. National providers serving your area are likely to depend on their network of local services, which may or may not be the best choice for your needs. In addition, some labor markets have more specialized agencies than others. Agencies in some labor markets do more training of their employees than agencies in other markets. Agency fees and services differ. Therefore, compare the abilities of external suppliers of contingent workers to your own ability to find, hire, and train contingent workers.

What Company Policies and Procedures Define Your Actions?

Company policies sometimes rule contingent staffing choices when they shouldn't, but do anyway. Head count drives lots of employment decisions in companies that measure staffing levels in terms of "heads" rather than hours worked. If your budget allows for contingent workers from outside the company, but you can't get authorization to employ people inside the company, then your contingent workers are going to be agency temporaries, leased employees, or independent contractors, not part-time employees or direct-hire temporaries who are on the payroll.

These days, it is commonplace to control head count by placing a freeze on hiring, but allowing services of contingent workers to be purchased as needed. The employment level surely stays down, and employment costs might stay down, although overhead expenditures might not. A system that counts personnel in terms of full-time equivalents allows the expansion of part-time employment, including part-timers working on a casual basis, because it permits two half-time employees to be counted as one full-time employee. Such a system is less biased in favor of external contingents.

Another aspect of policy that can influence the choice of contingent staffing option is the company's wage and salary structure. If you want to pay less *or* more to a contingent worker than the position description and job grade permit for an internal employee, you may need to seek an employee from the outside.

What Are Your Organization's Culture and Traditions?

If your company believes in performing most functions in-house and "growing its own" staff, it is likely to want contingent workers who are employees of the company. If it strives to be in the vanguard as a "virtual corporation," it may be biased toward using external contingent workers. Some managers who see temporaries from agencies only as fill-ins for absent secretaries may be biased against getting high-level contingent professionals from agencies. These built-in predispositions subconsciously influence the staffing option chosen for contingent workers.

More thoughtfully, some companies have strongly held values about how to treat people who work at the company. At Hewlett-Packard (HP), for example, the reasoning runs like this: If people are hired into the company as contingent workers and then let go when they are not needed—even if this is well understood by the employees at the time of employment—the displaced employee probably is left with no immediate good employment option. On the other hand, if HP gets contingent workers from help supply firms that do a good job of training their people and providing benefits for them, then when the contingent workers are no longer needed at HP, they have a good chance at quick reemployment elsewhere if they want it. Therefore, when all else is more or less equal, HP chooses temporaries from staffing companies as its contingent worker staffing option.

Managing a Mixed Workforce of Core and Contingent Workers

Since most companies have contingent workers, and most companies need temporaries, part-timers, or contract workers to give them flexibility, your company probably includes a mix of contingent workers and regular employees. How is this mixed workforce best managed? Strategic issues that require decisions include:

- How many contingent workers do we want?
- Are contingent workers expected to do the same or different jobs from regular employees?
- How long do we want contingent workers to stay with us?
- Can we get some flexibility from our regular employees as well as from our contingent workers?

In the pages that follow, we offer guidelines to help managers make these decisions in their own work units. (In Chapter 6, we take up several more micro, tactical issues about managing the contingent workers themselves.)

How Many Contingent Workers?

When asked how many contingent workers is the right number for a work unit, an experienced observer is likely to say that it might be less than one percent or it might be more than 90 percent. Another observer is likely to say that this question is not the first or most important one to ask. Neither observation is very helpful. What do you say when someone in the chairman's office asks you how large the company's contingent workforce ought to be? What do you do when a vice president says that the company ought to have 15 percent contingent workers? These scenarios do happen; we have to be prepared.

At Hewlett-Packard, the number of contingent workers companywide in the United States should not go above 10 to 15 percent; the actual number is around 7 percent. A company in the life insurance business estimates that about 14 percent of its employees are contingent workers and says that is a good number. Nationwide, the number of contingent workers can only be guessed at, but one guess (see Chapter 1) is that the number is about 20 to 25 percent of all employment.

But we need to know how many contingent workers to use in a work unit, not a companywide or national average. In the companies we have studied, contingent workers often make up a quarter to a third of the work unit population, although we have also encountered units with less than 10 percent and more than 50 percent.

The difficult part of knowing how many contingent workers to use is that it really does depend on the work setting. It is situation-specific. Earlier in this chapter, we gave examples of how different purposes for contingent workers determine different numbers of them to be used. The best we can do is to know the conditions that drive the optimum numbers of contingent workers up or down.

The number of contingent workers that can be used optimally in a work unit tends to go up if:

- Fluctuations in workload are large, short-cycle, or unpredictable.
- The work unit is sensitive to upturns and downturns in business conditions.
- The work unit is soon to be phased out or the type of work is about to change.
- Head count restrictions prevent additional hiring, but other costs are permitted.
- Work needs can be met with an ample supply of people who have the right skills and work habits.

- Compensation rates can be lower than for regular employees.
- Human resources management for employees is seen as burdensome or costly in money or time.

On the other hand, the number of contingent workers in a work unit needs to be kept down if:

- The work is done in teams where low turnover, shared responsibility, and mutual trust are key conditions.
- The corporate culture places significant value on commitment to the company or at least to the workplace.
- The complexity, sensitivity, or critical nature of the work requires a close relationship between employer and worker.

Looking across these conditions as they apply to your work unit, plus discerning other special features of how work is done in your unit, will lead to a ballpark range for the optimum number of contingent workers to use.

Should Contingent Workers Do the Same Jobs as Core Employees?

Of all the questions about structuring a contingent workforce, this one is the coin with two sides. Persuasive reasons can be advanced for saying yes and for saying no. And as a matter of fact, some companies use contingent workers in both ways in different work units. Their answer *is* yes and no.

Sometimes this question is subsidiary to the more important issue of the business purpose served by contingent workers. For example, if you use contingent workers to match the workforce to the workload, then you put contingent workers on the jobs that need to be expanded and contracted, supplementing the work of regular employees doing these jobs during peak times. They work together. This was the case in the bank backroom operations described earlier in this chapter and summarized in Figure 3-2.

If you have free choice about using contingent workers side-by-side with regular employees or not, then a case can be made for not doing so. (Legal counsel often recommends such job segregation; legal issues are discussed in more detail in Chapter 7.) The basic premise is that contingent workers do not have the same status and privileges as regular employees. If that premise holds, then you want to separate contingent workers in some fashion. One way to do that is to ensure that contingent workers do different jobs from core employees. Or if they do the same jobs, you ensure that their assignment is strictly bounded by time or purpose. For example, contingent workers can work side-by-side with core employees doing exactly the same jobs if they are both in a unit that is being phased out over the next, say, six months, or if they are working on a special project or a single big order.

On the contrary, if contingent and core employees do the same jobs in the same work unit indefinitely, then the following types of situations can arise, as related by managers in two different companies:

> We had some contingent workers on design and development and some core employees on maintenance, and we had a rebellion on our hands. Employees themselves look at what is interesting work or valuable work, and there is an expectation that core employees have dibs on those good jobs.

> The CEO gave all employees one day off and a bonus of $250 as a reward for successfully coming through the merger. Some agency temps wrote to him, asking to be included because they also had contributed to the successful merger. He said no, but he encouraged the agencies to give bonuses to their best people, and he funded the agencies to do that.

So a company can get trouble from either its core employees or its contingent workers if they both work together and yet are treated differently. The problem of the core-contingent relationship can be reversed. What about independent contractors who come in to a high-level project with superior specialized skills, and where the regular employees are inferior in experience and expertise? In this case, the regular employees feel threatened by the more productive contingent workers if both do the same type of work. Sometimes, too, the contingent worker may be chosen for a new job opening in the unit in which he or she works, causing resentment among core staff.

The lesson is this: If contingent workers are unequal to core employees in status and in the rights and privileges they enjoy, then continuing use of contingent workers in the same jobs in the same work unit side-by-side with regular employees is asking for trouble. Differentiation in function, purpose, or time frame of work is advisable.

This conclusion calls into question the basic premise with which we started. If contingent workers are treated on a more or less equitable basis with regular employees—for example, in wages and benefits—then the tension that could ensue from working closely together is not likely to arise. This issue is taken up in Chapter 6.

Flexibility From the Core?

Getting the flexibility to add and subtract labor input quickly does not have to be limited to the contingent workforce. The core workforce is an obvious second source of flexibility, potentially. Whether it is in actual practice is another question. For this discussion, we set aside the traditional practices of overtime and layoffs, and ask instead what other ways there are to get flexibility from regular employees. Because you don't expect to add and subtract people from the core, you instead look into changing the number of hours they work, or you change the work they do.

Part-Timers With Variable Hours

The regular part-time employees you have in your core workforce who probably work between 20 and 30 hours a week on the average appear to be candidates for varying their hours of work up or down as your need for them changes. Some companies routinely do this. But there are limits. An East Coast insurance company manager put it like this:

> We find that most people are part-time because they have other things in their life—they go to school, they have the baby-sitter, they run the carpool, they have another schedule they're trying to meet. They can't make sudden adjustments.

Most people, especially people who do entry-level jobs, need structure and stability in their work life. If they can't change the schedules of schools and spouses that dictate their schedule outside of work, you can't expect them to change their work schedule for you. Most people also need to know their exact income because they have financial commitments, and if you pay them by the hour and change their hours, their salaries will vary. So the question comes down to this: Can you get regular part-timers who are able to flex? If so, hire them with the understanding that their hours will vary. If not, try another scheduling option with regular full-time employees.

Full-Timers With Variable Hours

Two types of alternative schedules for regular full-time (or part-time) employees give flexibility in hours worked: work sharing and annual hours. Work sharing means that all the employees in a work unit adjust their work hours down from their usual full-time hours when work is slack. It is often used as an alternative to layoffs in Europe. For example, Volkswagen (VW) in Germany used work sharing in 1994 when faced with falling car sales. VW, with agreement from its workers, cut weekly hours from 36 to 29 (about 20 percent), and the company and its employees shared equally in the financial outcome (employees lost 10 percent of their gross earnings and VW paid 10 percent higher hourly wage rates).[11] In the United States, work sharing has been used sparingly, in part because in most states partial unemployment compensation is not paid to work sharers. Nevertheless, the idea behind work sharing—that all employees share in the ups and downs of working time—might be implemented in some work units in which the core-ring model is rejected.

Annual hours is another practice that is increasingly used in Europe (9 percent of the British workforce has this schedule, and more than that in Germany and France).[12] In an annual hours schedule, the time unit is the year, not the week. For example, 2,000 hours (or 1,500 hours) are distributed over 12 months rather than 40 hours (or 30 hours) distributed over one week. According to Paul Radly, employee relations manager for Railtrack (the British state-owned rail infrastructure company), annual hours ". . . would give us enormous flexibility in matching employees' hours to service needs, eliminate excessive premium payments for overtime, and give us greater freedom in changing daily working time patterns" (as reported in the *Financial Times*, September 23, 1994).

However, it is not clear that employees prefer annual hours. Railtrack has not even brought forward annual hours as a bargaining item with its union. The same question as before is encountered: Are regular core employees able to adjust their work hours quickly? The answer depends on the make-up of the workforce in your specific work unit.

Variable Work Assignments

If you can't vary the hours of work that regular employees put in, then maybe you can vary the work they do—you try to achieve functional flexibility as a partial substitute for numerical flexibility. This plan is feasible if you have a work unit in which peak demand for one type of work is accompanied by slack demand for another type of work. If you do, and if some of your employees are cross-trained or multiskilled, then you shift those employees from areas of slack to areas of peak demand.

Endnotes

1. The first excerpt is from William Bridges, "The End of the Job," *Fortune,* September 19, 1994, pp. 64–74; the second is from Shari Caudron, "Contingent Work Force Spurs HR Planning," *Personnel Journal,* July 1994, pp. 52–60.
2. A Survey by The Conference Board provides new data on company experiences with contingent labor. See Helen Axel, "Contingent Employment," *HR Executive Review,* vol. 3, no. 2 (1995).
3. Atkinson's core-ring model is described in an article published in the August 1984 issue of *Personnel Management* called "Manpower Strategies for Flexible Organizations." Control Data Corporation's similar model was part of its business plan.
4. This and other evidence reported here is from Helen Axel, "Downsizing," *HR Executive Review,* vol. 1, no. 1 (New York: The Conference Board, 1993).
5. This report is based on the authors' paper "Downsizing and Flexibility" presented at the May 1994 meeting of the International Society for Work Options, Amersfoort, Netherlands.
6. The source is the American Management Association. "Survey Highlights: 1993 AMA Survey on Downsizing and Assistance to Displaced Workers," news release, September 23, 1993.
7. See the citations in Wayne Cascio, "Downsizing: What Do We Know?

What Have We Learned?" *Academy of Management Executive,* vol. 7, no. 1 (1993).

8. A. A. Johnson and F. Linden, *Availability of a Quality Workforce,* Report No. 1010 (New York: The Conference Board, 1992).

9. For discussions of the reasons for downsizing, see Cascio (note 7) and K. S. Cameron, S. J. Freeman, and A. K. Mishra, "Best Practices in White-Collar Downsizing: Managing Contradictions," *Academy of Management Executive,* vol. 5, no. 3 (1991).

10. See *Creating a Flexible Workplace* by Barney Olmsted and Suzanne Smith, published in 1995 in its second edition by AMACOM Books, for an encyclopedic but readable description of these and other scheduling and staffing options.

11. This information comes from communication from Andreas Hoff, a Berlin consultant on work schedules.

12. These data and the information on Britain's Railtrack are reported in the *Financial Times,* September 23, 1994.

3

Does Contingent Labor Cost Less? Tools to Get the Answer

"And cost-conscious companies are turning to a contingent workforce—part-timers, temporaries, contract labor—to avoid soaring fringe benefits and to increase profits."

The Wall Street Journal, March 10, 1993

"Contingent workers cost an estimated 20 percent to 40 percent less than core employees."

The Wall Street Journal, March 11, 1993

If you ask the average manager why his or her company uses contingent workers, chances are that one answer, and probably the first answer, is that they are cheaper than regular employees. That is what we read in the business press. That is what managers tell us. Companies use temporary and part-time workers partly because they keep labor costs down.

That is also what we train managers to think. For example, a series of two-day conferences in May, June, and July 1994 sponsored by the American Management Association on the topic of "How to Choose and Manage Alternative Employer/Employee Relationships" included in its course outline a section on the benefits of flexible staffing. The flexible staffing methods discussed at these conferences were contingent labor, contract labor, employee leasing, and temporary help.

The clear thrust of this section of the conference according to its promotional literature was on how these staffing methods can help businesses cut labor costs and cut human resources management tasks as well. Of the nine topics listed in this section of the conference program, four were directly targeted to cost savings; they featured the words ''expenses'' and ''costs.'' The other five topics approached cost savings indirectly. (See Figure 3-1.) See also the coursebook prepared for the conference by its leader, Jeffrey S. Klein, for a complete picture of the content of the conference.

Is it true that contingent labor cuts costs? And if it is true, where do the cost cuts come from?

Contingent Workers Can Save Money for Your Company

If many managers, journalists, and trainers believe that contingent labor costs less than core employment, there must be something to it. Three sources of cost savings are available: (1) wages and benefits, (2) flexibility, and (3) management time.

Figure 3-1. How a management conference sees the benefits of flexible staffing.

How Flexible Staffing Can Help Your Company: Identifying and Quantifying the Benefits

1. Allows for staff size flexibility to meet variations in demand
2. Keeps payroll expenses under control—or even reduces them
3. Streamlines recruiting, administration, and HR expenses
4. Alleviates certain federal and state compliance responsibilities
5. Diminishes the risk of employment-related litigation
6. Controls and reduces health insurance costs
7. Reallocates resources toward sales, marketing, and management
8. Permits hiring from a pool of tried-and-true workers
9. Allows for quantifying cost savings using operational/productivity measurements and analytical techniques

---

Source: Adapted from American Management Association conference brochure.

Less Pay, No Benefits

Take another look at the business press for clues. The cover story in the January 24, 1994, issue of *Fortune* magazine was entitled, "The Contingency Workforce." The second sentence of this article said of the part-timers, freelancers, subcontractors, and independent professionals who make up the contingency workforce that "They're . . . usually paid less and almost never receive benefits." This point quickly becomes self-evident: If you pay lower wages to contingent workers or give them few or no benefits, your payroll cost goes down.

Benefits

The benefits cost of contingent workers will almost always be lower than for regular workers if the contingent workers are not employees of the company. Agency temporaries and independent contractors are not employees of the company where they work (however, see Chapter 7 on legal issues for exceptions to this rule). Therefore, that company does not need to pay statutory benefits that are legally required for its other employees, such as social security, unemployment insurance, disability insurance, and workers' compensation. These are all payroll taxes that can be avoided. Since temporary workers are employees of the agency that supplies them, the agency pays these statutory benefits.

What's more, the company does not need to offer any of the other expensive benefits such as health insurance, life insurance, retirement plans, or any paid leaves that usually are given to regular employees. It's entirely a matter of company choice, and since benefits costs have been escalating so rapidly in recent years, this is an obvious target for cost saving.

Keep in mind that certain temporary help agencies pay selected optional benefits as well as the legally required employment taxes to some of their people. However, these agency-provided benefits usually are earned through length of service with the agency so that "regular" temporaries are favored just as regular core employees are favored.

The company that gets workers from an agency pays a fee to the agency above and beyond the wage rate that the worker gets. This fee also includes the agency's costs of recruiting, screening, and training its people. In the end, the question is whether or not the total payment to the agency is less than the company's usual wage and benefits cost for regular employees. The same *Fortune* magazine article cited above goes on to say that "The bill [from staffing companies] to corporate clients can run as much as 50 percent above a regular worker's hourly wage, though smart managers can whittle that premium to as low as 20 percent. . . ."

For independent short-term contractors who are not supplied by an agency but rather located by the company itself, there is no agency fee. These people are generally paid out of expense vouchers just as purchases of supplies or reimbursement for travel are paid for, and they do not need to receive any benefits either.

Part-time workers who are in the contingent workforce often are employees of the company where they work, on the payroll. Unlike with temporaries or short-term contractors, the company pays legally required employment taxes. These employees are also covered by other labor regulations, especially ERISA (Employee Retirement Income Security Act) if they work 1,000 hours or more in a year (about 20 hours a week). In this case, they must be given access to the same pension benefits that full-time employees receive, prorated to time worked, of course. What this means, practically, is that most part-timers who are contingent workers put in less than 20 hours a week so that the company does not in fact have to pay them any benefits beyond statutory benefits. For example, according to 1993 data from the U.S. Bureau of Labor Statistics, only 15 percent of all part-time workers receive employer-provided group health insurance as opposed to 64 percent of full-time workers.

Wages

How much contingent workers are paid is a choice of the managers in the company that uses them, affected by prevailing wage rates from the labor market and, in the case of agency temporaries, the fees charged by the agency. Most managers want to contain the wage rates they pay their workers. (But not all want to pay the lowest possible wages—some managers believe in the economists' concept of "efficiency wages," which basically says that if you pay more, you get more, turning on its head most psychologists' concept that reward follows performance.) Still, no one pays more than needed to get good people. So the question is whether it is routinely possible to get good contingent workers for less than good core employees.

The outside factor that influences this choice is the labor market, where wage rates are determined by forces of supply and demand. It is well known that part-time employees earn smaller wages than full-time employees. In 1989, hourly-paid part-timers earned $4.83 on the average while hourly-paid full-timers earned $7.83. Temporaries from agencies earned $7.59 an hour. (These statistics come from U.S. government sources; complete citations are given in Table 6-2.) Bear in mind that this comparison controls for some job differences because it is restricted to hourly-wage workers and thus does not include high-salary, full-time managers and professionals.

Nevertheless, some of this wage gap can be explained by the differences in the jobs that core employees and contingent workers do. For example, 43 percent of all temporaries work in administrative support jobs while only 17 percent of the overall labor force is in these jobs (as reported in Chapter 2). Part-time employees are concentrated in sales, service, and administrative support positions—and these are relatively low-wage jobs.

In addition, both part-timers and temporaries are quite a bit younger on the average than the rest of the workforce. More than half of all part-timers and temporaries are younger than 35, and among temporaries alone fully one-third are younger than 25. Only one-fifth of regular workers are that young (more details are given in Chapter 6). Young workers have less experience and so they are paid less.

Can you pay part-timers or temporaries a lower hourly rate than full-timers or core employees when they all do the same job? Yes, you can if there are more people available for part-time or temporary work than there are jobs to fill. Supply that exceeds demand puts downward pressure on wages. While there is no way to measure supply-demand balance directly, one indicator of it is the unemployment rate. And here we know that more part-timers are unemployed than full-timers (see Table 3-1).

Part-time unemployment is exacerbated by the tendency of companies to eliminate part-time jobs first during downturns; some of these jobholders are contingent workers. More unemployment means diminished ability of jobholders or job applicants to get higher wages. Companies can probably pay less to part-timers than full-timers if they want to.

Even if there were no difference in unemployment rates between contingent workers and regular employees, there is another reason why contingent workers might often be paid smaller wages. If the

Table 3-1. Unemployment rates of part-time and full-time workers.

Year	Part-Time (percentages)	Full-Time (percentages)
1994	7.1	6.8
1993	7.4	7.4
1992	9.2	7.1
1991	8.3	6.5
1990	7.4	5.2
1989	7.4	4.9

Note: 1994 data are not directly comparable with 1993 data.
Source: U.S. Bureau of Labor Statistics, *Monthly Labor Review,* various issues.

people who are available for part-time or temporary work have no or few other options and cannot bargain for higher wage rates, they have scarcely any market power and must accept the wage that is offered to them. Since a substantial share of all part-time workers are involuntary (about 40 percent), they have no other employment choice, and they have little market power. Among temporary workers from agencies, about a third of the important reasons they give for being temporary workers reflect lack of choice—"It's a way to get full-time work," "I'm between full-time jobs," or "I'm new to the area." (See Table 3-2.) These people might have to accept low wages because they have few alternatives.

Match the Workforce to the Workload

The second way that the use of contingent workers might result in lower costs and increased profits is that companies may now continuously adjust the size of their workforce to the size of their workload. Contingent workers provide numerical flexibility. Managers can add contingent workers day-by-day as needed, and managers can cut workers just as quickly. Because they let companies match workforce to workload, contingent workers avoid the wasted cost of idle people during slack times and the extra cost of overtime during peak periods.

An advertising campaign featured in national business magazines by Olsten Corporation, a temporary services company, put it this way:

Table 3-2. Reasons why people are temporary workers.

Reasons to Be a Temporary Worker	Percentage of all Reasons
Reasons that reflect lack of choice: A way to get full-time work, between full-time jobs, new to area	31
Reasons that are neutral about preference for temporary work: Get additional income, improve skills	32
Reasons that reflect preference for temporary work: Flexible work time, less stress, can't work full-time, need time for children	37

Source: Calculated from survey by National Association of Temporary and Staffing Services, 1989.

The Secret to Increased Profits . . .

Today your business is one thing. Tomorrow it could be a whole different animal. Which means you need a staff that can restructure with it. Because while your employees are your most valuable asset, they're also your biggest expense. Olsten has the solution: flexibility. With Olsten's Flexible Workforce™ you maintain a core of full-time workers. Then, depending on workload, you obtain additional temporary workers from Olsten only when you need them. As a result, your company is always at its leanest, yet ready for anything. Because you're never understaffed or overstaffed, you eliminate the enormous expense of overtime . . .

Fluctuations in workload can be short term (hour-by-hour or day-by-day) or long term, over the several years of a business cycle that may shift from peak of growth to nadir of recession. Fluctuations are sometimes quite predictable, like the seasonal pattern of some consumer products, or they may be totally unpredictable, like the uneven bunching of orders for some industrial products.

To show how contingent workers are added and subtracted according to predictable seasonal fluctuations in workload, look at the experience of a manufacturing and distribution facility of a consumer products company, shown in Figure 3-2.

Figure 3-2. Workload and contingent labor over time.

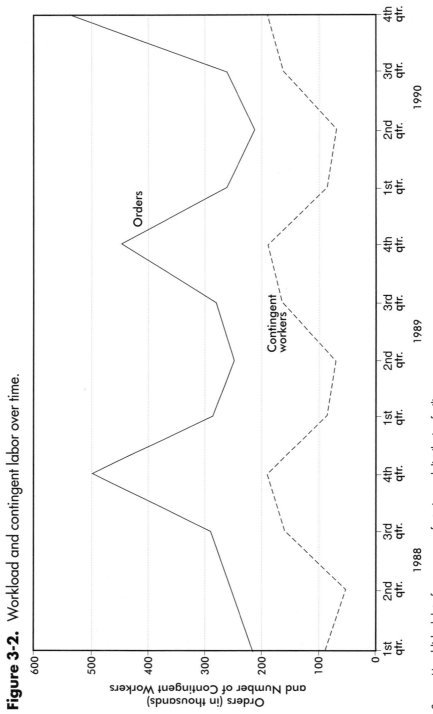

Orders

Contingent
workers

Orders (in thousands)
and Number of Contingent Workers

1st
qtr.

2nd
qtr.

3rd
qtr.

4th
qtr.

1st
qtr.

2nd
qtr.

3rd
qtr.

4th
qtr.

1st
qtr.

2nd
qtr.

3rd
qtr.

4th
qtr.

1988

1989

1990

0

100

200

300

400

500

600

Source: Unpublished data from one manufacturing and distribution facility.

Orders shoot up every fourth quarter, and correspondingly, managers increase the number of contingent workers in the company from a low of about 50 people in the slack second quarter to a high of nearly 200 people in the peak fourth quarter. Overtime is also used in the fourth quarter, but less than it would be without the contingent workers, thus saving lots of money in premium pay. Because most of the contingent workers aren't there during the slack periods, the payroll is trimmed when the orders are down.

Cutbacks in Management Time

The third way in which the use of a contingent workforce might lower company costs is that managers may be able to eliminate some unwanted management tasks. It is hard to put a price tag on this potential cost saving. Yet it is a powerful force in favor of contingent workers because it directly and personally affects both operating managers and human resources managers.

Cuts in Functions

Some of the avoided management tasks are actually functions that do not have to be performed for contingent workers because they are not regular employees. If the contingent workers are temporary workers from a help supply service, you don't have to do any recruiting or selecting. You might be able to get by with less training (but read more on this important issue in a later section of this chapter about training and other fixed costs). You don't have to do any formal performance appraisal (though you might want to informally evaluate work efficiency and achievement). There is no career development because these people are not career employees. You don't need to provide services such as employee assistance programs, child care referral, or even company picnics. You might even offload some of the usual supervisory tasks if you have an on-site representative of the agency that supplies your temporary workers. In other words, using temporary workers frees you from the chores of hiring, firing, and lots of other things in between. If the contingent workers are part-timers who are employees, you still avoid some of these management tasks.

Cuts in Overhead

Some of the potential cost saving from contingent workers, above and beyond eliminating certain management functions, involves eliminating accounting for, reporting on, and keeping track of these employees. Contingent workers entail less paperwork than core employees. They cut down on the detested personnel overhead (but might shift some overhead to the purchasing department). For example, wage and salary administration is easier, reporting on compliance with a range of government-mandated programs is easier, and documentation of performance is not necessary. As one manager in an electronics assembly operation said of the work done by his agency temporaries, "If I don't like one of these guys, I just tell the agency not to send him back tomorrow."

From the company's perspective, what is going on here is the outsourcing of part of the human resources management function itself. Recruiting, selection, some training, maybe some supervision, and possibly even some other services are provided by the contingent worker's employer rather than by the client company itself. At the extreme, the contingent workers belong to an employee leasing company that manages *all* the human resources needs of its workers. The contingent workers in turn can be regarded by the company where they work as similar to an outsourced component for the assembly of a finished product. If someone else can make the product or supply the service better or cheaper than you can, then buy it from them. If your core competence is not personnel administration, why not let someone else do it?

The Flip Side: How the Savings Can Disappear

Every story has two sides. If employing contingent workers can cut costs for the company, it can also raise costs. The aforementioned *Fortune* magazine cover story of January 24, 1994, reports experiences of managers: "Some also insist that excessive reliance on temporary outsiders can drag productivity down, not up." The American Management Association conferences on "How to Choose and Manage Alternative Employer/Employee Relationships," also cited earlier in this chapter, examine supervisors' concerns about inefficiencies, losing control, getting loyalty and teamwork, protecting proprietary information, maintaining corporate culture, "two-tier" inequity, and developing future managers (see Figure 3-3).

Taking these and other concerns into consideration, you need a framework for analyzing the downside risk of contingent labor. You need to ask how temporary and part-time workers might perversely add to labor costs rather than reduce them. Then you need a way to balance out the pluses and minuses and come up with a "net" figure for the labor cost story for contingent workers. The two key variables are productivity and training.

Productivity, Not Just Wages

As we have seen, one of the ways in which the utilization of contingent labor might be less expensive than core labor is that it reduces wages and benefits. But no business seeks to minimize wages. Instead, businesses try to minimize costs—and ultimately to maximize profits or earnings per share or growth or market share, or to achieve a target rate of return on investment.

Labor cost does not depend on wages and benefits alone. It depends on productivity also. Low-wage labor can be high-cost if it is not productive, and conversely high-wage labor can be low-cost if it is highly productive. This lesson is well learned from international comparisons. A reason why relatively expensive American labor can

Figure 3-3. How a management conference sees the disadvantages of flexible staffing.

Typical Disadvantages: Recognizing the Detrimental Effects of Flexible Staffing

1. Limitations on identifying and training tomorrow's managers
2. Concerns regarding the creation of a "two-tier" workforce
3. Inefficiencies caused by unfamiliarity with corporate policies and procedures
4. Challenges to protecting proprietary information
5. Problems with engendering corporate loyalty and encouraging teamwork
6. Concerns about maintaining corporate culture and identity
7. Problems related to loss of control over employees

Source: Adapted from American Management Association conference brochure.

compete with relatively cheap British labor is because American labor is more productive. A reason why not all high-wage Western manufacturing moves to low-wage Eastern Europe or low-wage Asia is because labor is less productive there.

The key is *unit labor cost*. Add up how much you pay in labor— wages and benefits multiplied by time worked—and divide by how much you get from labor—quantity of output—and the result is unit labor cost. In other words:

$$\text{Unit labor cost} = (W \times L)/Q,$$

where W = wage and benefit rate per hour,
          L = hours worked, and
          Q = quantity of output produced per hour

Productivity is part of unit labor cost. If productivity is defined narrowly as output per unit of input, then unit labor cost goes up as productivity goes down because output/input goes down (less quantity of output for the same labor input gives you a smaller divisor in the unit labor cost equation and hence a larger number for unit labor cost).

Can contingent workers be as productive as core employees doing similar jobs? Of course the answer depends on particular circumstances, but you can get a general idea by looking at the factors that determine productivity.

Individual Productivity

The productivity of individual workers depends in the first place on their skill or ability to produce, and that depends on their human capital. The human capital embodied in a worker is built up over time from formal classroom education during youth, applied training in work-related skills as an adult, and experience from employment or "learning by doing."

Many contingent workers do not have as much human capital as their core employee counterparts simply because they do not have as much training or experience. They have less training and experience precisely because they are contingent workers—it's a vicious cycle. In contrast, some temporary and part-time workers are highly specialized professionals with sought-after technical skills, and they in turn may be even more productive than regular employees.

Individual productivity depends in the second place on effort. How hard people work is affected by what managers do interpersonally and by company policy. In the words of one discontented temporary worker, as quoted in *The Wall Street Journal*, March 11, 1993:

> It got to the point I hated to go to work. I hated who I worked for because I wasn't being paid or treated fairly. And I know I was less productive because I was so disheartened.

What can managers do to get people to work hard? This question is one of the most difficult that managers face. Some answers turn out to be dead ends. For example, we know from many disappointing experiences that a happy worker is not always a productive worker.

But some simple truths are self-evident. For instance, hard workers are usually motivated and committed. Motivation and commitment come from participation and involvement in the affairs of the workplace, a sense of employment security, and a belief that rewards are fair, among other things (see Gaertner and Nollen[1] for a discussion of commitment). A note of caution: None of this says that you cannot ever get good work out of unmotivated or uncommitted people; it says that motivation and commitment give you better odds of success.)

In many cases, contingent workers are unlikely to put forth as much effort as regular employees. Contingent workers can hardly be as involved in the workplace as core employees if they do not belong to it, and they cannot have a sense of job security because their contingent status rules that out by definition.

In other cases, commitment to the company surely does not matter. What if the job is routine, machine-paced, and highly structured? What scope is left for involvement or commitment? Some of the administrative support, sales, and service jobs that contingent workers do are like this. What if the worker prefers to be a contingent worker precisely because no corporate commitment is expected? On the opposite end of the job spectrum, what if the contingent worker belongs to a profession and focuses on the work itself, expressing loyalty to the profession to which he or she belongs?

In still other cases, the effort put forth by a contingent worker can top that of a regular employee. Remember that about two-thirds of all temporary workers are looking for regular employment out of their temporary stint and one-third or more get it (this information is reported further in Chapter 6). These people have a powerful motivation to work hard and do a good job while they are temporaries because their employment future depends on it. And finally, if the job is either stressful, as some high-tech specialties are, or repetitive, as some clerical and service jobs are, then maybe productivity is higher when the job is done in short spells by part-timers or temporaries.

Work Unit Performance: When Teamwork Counts

The individual output/input concept of productivity is not comprehensive enough. Although how much physical output one person produces is undeniably important, we also need to embrace a more broadly conceived measure: work unit performance. What the company needs in the income statement at the end of the year is performance from business units. The performance "whole" may not be the sum of its individual productivity "parts."

This issue was encountered recently by a large electronics company, one of whose operations was structured into work units of about 25 workers each, including "supplementals" (this is the company's term for temporary workers from a help supply service). The work was accomplished wholly in teams. A production manager in this company put it to the authors this way:

> You know, once we really got into this world-class manufacturing thing, we started to look at the supplementals. Sure, we want these folks because we don't ever again want to go through layoffs like we had 10 years ago. And we always thought they were cheaper anyway because we do pay the agencies nearly $1.50 less an hour than our own regular employees get, and they are good workers, there's no problem there at all. Now I'm not so sure we're doing the right thing. You see, with all these supplementals coming and going you get so much churn and it just makes it hard for the teams to work.

If output is produced by teams and team members have to work cooperatively together, then team membership needs to be fairly stable. Good individual productivity is not enough if group process is the key. (In fact, this company does not even conduct performance appraisals for its employees formally because output is produced by teams, not individuals.) Group process is disrupted when long-tenured people leave and new people join. This company became concerned that achieving its world-class performance goals would be jeopardized by damage done to teamwork owing to the ebb and flow of contingent workers.

Even if work is not done in teams, there are other potential adverse effects that contingent workers might have on work unit performance. The American Management Association conference program (in Figure 3-3) highlighted them. Managers do not have as much control over contingent workers as they do over regular employees; the detached relationship between company and worker goes both ways. Bringing in outside contract workers risks compromising proprietary information, with long-run competitive implications. Different treatment of core and contingent people who work side by side might divide the work unit into two tiers of favored and disadvantaged workers; tensions might develop. Attempts to build a corporate culture as a unifying and motivating force might be frustrated.

Training and Other Fixed Costs

What if the wages and benefits paid to contingent workers are less than the compensation paid to core employees, and what if their productivity is about as good (and there are no problems with teamwork or work unit performance)? Then their unit labor cost is definitely lower. But can we then say that contingent labor costs less than core labor?

Maybe. Even if the unit labor cost of contingent workers is less than for core employees, they can end up costing more because the cost of employing workers is more than the wages and benefits they are paid. Even though some management tasks are avoided with contingent workers, some remain. These additions are costs in areas such as recruiting and selecting (eliminated if done by a temporary help supply service—but then of course the agency gets a fee) and training, which is potentially quite a big cost even for contingent workers. On the other hand, overhead costs such as tools or space, or human resources managers' salaries, are already incurred on behalf of regular employees and do not change because of contingent workers, so you may consider them "free."

Training is an example of an additional employment cost beyond wages and benefits that is usually necessary to some extent even for contingent workers. All workers need some amount of initial orientation to the workplace, and most workers need some amount of training in how to do the job they are assigned. Some workers might need considerably more training to become proficient in the skills required. How much more depends on the availability of skills in the local labor market, and the degree to which help supply services can supply people with ready-to-go skills.

Training cost has the dual characteristics that it is incurred up front when the contingent worker is first brought in, and it is incurred per person, not per hour worked or per unit of output produced. Training is a fixed cost. In addition, training is an investment in the future productivity of workers. After training is completed, you expect to recover the investment: The value of the output that trained workers produce for the company should exceed the cost of their wages and benefits. This margin of what you get over what you pay is what allows the training cost to be recovered. But it takes time to recover the investment, and so the length of time after training that workers stay in their jobs or with the company is critical.[2] This is why some companies try to bind employees who get company-paid training through contracts. This is why poaching of newly trained workers from other companies is frowned on.

In the case of contingent labor, it is easy to see that training is a potential cost problem. Contingent workers do not stay in the job a long time; they wouldn't be contingent workers if they did (with the exception of some notorious unintended instances of "permanent" temporaries). Therefore, the company doesn't have much time to get its training investment recovered. And what if it is not recovered? Then it just becomes an additional cost of employment, as if wages were higher or more benefits were paid.

Training Cost Components: How They Add Up

To take a closer look at the cost of training, see the diagram in Figure 3-4. This diagram illustrates the types of training that might be undertaken and how the costs are incurred (you might not do all types or incur all costs):

- *Initial classroom orientation and training*, which might be provided for as little as a half-day or as long as a few weeks.

Figure 3-4. Cost of training and training cost recovery.

A. Classroom Training

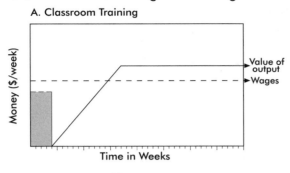

B. On-the-Job Training

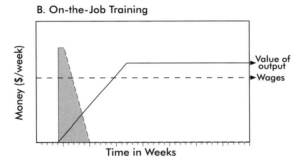

C. Opportunity Cost

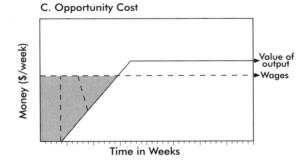

D. Training Cost Recovery

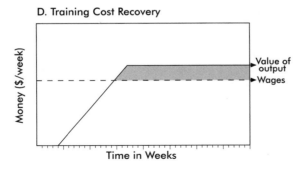

—*Direct costs,* including salary of a trainer and rental costs of facilities (training room and equipment). See the shaded area in Panel A in Figure 3-4.

—*Opportunity cost,* which consists of wages paid to the trainee while no output is being produced. See part of the shaded area in Panel C in Figure 3-4.

- *On-the-job training,* which may be given by a supervisor or an experienced co-worker for as little as a half-day or as long as several weeks.

—*Direct cost,* mainly scrappage (defective output or wasted materials). Not shown in Figure 3-4 (assumed to be zero).

—*Opportunity costs,* defined as the value of the supervisor's lost output (the shaded area in Panel B in Figure 3-4), and the difference between what the trainee is paid and the value of his or her output (part of the shaded area in Panel C in Figure 3-4).

- *Learning-by-doing,* which will continue with little or no attention from a supervisor until the worker achieves a productivity level that reaches company standards.

—*Opportunity cost,* defined as the difference between what the trainee is paid and the value of his or her output. See part of the shaded area in Panel C in Figure 3-4.

- *Continuing education or training,* which might be provided periodically during the year in new technical fields or in workplace relations topics; it might be either classroom or on-the-job training, and its costs are figured using the same methods described above. Not shown in Figure 3-4 (assumed to be zero).

Recovering Training Costs: The Time Factor

After classroom training, on-the-job training, and learning-by-doing are all completed and the worker has achieved the expected productivity level, the company can begin to recover its training investment. The output produced by the trained worker should have more value to the company than the wages and benefits that the company pays the worker. This is the shaded area in Panel D in Figure 3-4. If this margin does not exist, there is no way to get training costs back, and training has to be seen as something other than an investment in productivity. Notice that Area D is open-ended to the right—the longer the worker stays in the job or with the company, the bigger Area D gets, and the bigger the company's return on its training investment. Time on the job is a critical variable. Not even the world's greatest training can be a good investment unless the worker stays on the job or at least in the company and produces output for a while. If the worker leaves too soon, the cost is not paid back, and you have to repeat the training cost for the next new worker. Of course, new core employees need training also, but they ordinarily stay on the job much longer than contingent workers, so training cost recovery is less of a problem for core workers.

This leads to a fundamental dilemma and a serious management problem: Unless training is nothing more than token orientation, contingent workers must stay on the job a reasonable length of time in order for it to pay off. Yet contingent workers by definition have no attachment to the company and are not expected or even permitted to stay on the job a long time. They come and go at managers' discretion and of their own volition. Training for contingent workers is likely to be an extra cost of employment.

Cost-Effectiveness

If training or other fixed employment costs are not fully recovered, they are extra costs of using contingent workers. Does this mean that contingent labor is more expensive than regular employees? Maybe. To find out, you need the last link in the chain: cost-effectiveness. If contingent workers have lower unit labor cost than core employees, you need to net the extra cost of contingent workers—their unrecovered training cost—against their unit labor cost saving. It is possible that the lower wages and benefits paid to contingent workers after training more than offset the extra training cost. Or the balance could go the other way. Each case has to be figured out on the basis of its own unique numbers. (The Appendix to this chapter provides details.)

If the balance goes against contingent workers—if they cost more in total than core employees—then the inescapable conclusion is that the flexibility they provide comes at a price.

Summing Up: What Managers Need to Know

The question in this chapter is: Are contingent workers cheaper than core employees? The answer is that it depends—on wages and benefits, productivity, training costs, and time on the job. Each of these factors can be assessed for the unique features of each different work setting. But some general tendencies can be pointed out:

- Wages can be lower and benefits can be fewer for contingent workers compared to core employees in most cases. The labor market functions to push down wages for contingent workers. Benefits are costly and not legally required for contingent workers who are not employees.
- Individual productivity for contingent workers is likely to be less than for core employees, and work unit performance may be hampered in settings where teamwork matters. Contingent workers probably have less human capital and commitment, and they tend to join and leave work units frequently.
- Unit labor cost of contingent workers compared to core employees can go either way.
- Training that is required for new contingent workers is likely to be an extra cost of contingent labor. Training costs are not likely to be recovered because contingent workers do not stay on the job very long.
- The cost-effectiveness of contingent labor versus core employees is uncertain. It depends on a lower unit labor cost of contingent labor outweighing the extra training cost.

Whether or not contingent workers save money for a company is difficult to calculate and is of course different for each business. Thus, you should also consider the saving in management time that contingent labor permits, although that, too, is hard to quantify. More importantly, if contingent workers are used to better match the size of the workforce to the amount of work to be done, even extra training costs and higher total labor costs may well be worth the price in exchange for the flexibility that contingent labor provides.

Endnotes

1. Karen Gaertner, and Stanley Nollen, "Career Experiences, Perceptions of Employment Practices, and Psychological Commitment to the Organization," *Human Relations* 42, 11 (1989), pp. 975–991.
2. The concept of training as an investment in human capital was developed

by Gary S. Becker, who published a book, *Human Capital*, in 1964 and who later won a Nobel Prize in economics, and by Jacob Mincer (1962), whose ideas can be found in his article "On-the-Job Training: Costs, Returns, and Some Implications," *Journal of Political Economy*, 70, 5, part II (October 1962), pp. 50–79. This brief explanation summarizes their detailed expositions.

Appendix: How to Determine Numerically the Cost-Effectiveness of Contingent Labor

The following three tables, with definitions, formulas, and explanatory notes, are intended to help managers determine whether or not contingent labor is cheaper than core employment in their work unit. Table 3-3 lays out the calculation of unit labor cost (or alternatively, a pay/performance ratio). Table 3-4 shows how to calculate the costs of training. Table 3-5 shows how to determine if training costs are recovered and how to compare unrecovered training costs, if any, to unit labor cost savings, if any.

Table 3-3. How to determine unit labor cost for contingent and core workers.

	A Variable	B Contingent	C Core
1	Compensation, $/hr. (Rows 2 + 3 + 4)		
2	Wage rate, $/hr.		
3	Benefits rate, $/hr.*		
4	Agency fee, $/hr.*		
5	Productivity		
6	Output rate, units/hr.		
7	Performance appraisal		
8	Unit labor cost, $/unit (Rows 1 ÷ 6)		
9	Pay/performance ratio (Rows 1 ÷ 7)		

To determine the percentage difference between core employees and contingent workers on each variable, make the following calculations:

Compensation:	B1 − C1 =
Productivity:	B6 − C6 =
Performance appraisal:	B7 − C7 =
Unit labor cost:	B8 − C8 =
Pay/performance ratio:	B9 − C9 =

*The benefits rate may be zero if contingent workers are supplied by an agency or no benefits are paid. The agency fee will be zero if contingent workers are employees not supplied from an agency. If no output/input measure is available for productivity because of the nature of the work, use performance appraisal data instead. If no performance appraisal data are available, adopt alternative "what if" assumptions about productivity differences. The end result you obtain will be either unit labor cost difference *or* pay/performance ratio difference between contingent workers and core employees.

Table 3-4. How to determine training cost for contingent workers.

	Variable (measured as $/trainee)	Cost
1	Formal classroom training (Rows 2 + 3 + 4)	
2	Direct cost of trainer	
3	Direct cost of facilities	
4	Opportunity cost (trainee's compensation)	
5	On-the-job training (Rows 6 + 7)	
6	Direct cost of scrappage	
7	Opportunity cost Supervisor's lost output Trainee's compensation less output	
8	Total cost of training (Rows 1 + 5)	

Note: The company expects to get value of output from workers equal to the amount it pays workers. To determine value of output, equate output rate to compensation rate for entry-level core employee or trained contingent worker.

Table 3-5. How to determine cost-effectiveness of contingent labor.

	Variable	Figure
1	Unit labor cost (from Table 3-3, B8 − C8) *or* Pay/performance ratio (from Table 3-3, B9 − C9)	
2	Training cost unrecovered, $/trainee [Table 3-4, Row 8 − this Table, Rows (3x4)]	
3	Training cost recovery rate, $/hr. (value of output less compensation)	
4	Time on job after training, hrs.	
5	Contingent labor cost saving after training, $/worker (unit labor cost difference × hours worked)	
6	Total cost difference for contingent workers, $/worker (Rows 2 − 5)	

Decision Methodology:
1. If unit labor costs or pay/performance ratio (Row 1) is higher for contingent workers, they are not cost-effective.
2. If unit labor cost or pay/performance ratio is lower for contingent labor, see if training cost is unrecovered (Row 2).
   a. If no training costs are unrecovered (Row 2), contingent workers are cost-effective.
   b. If some training costs are unrecovered, determine total cost difference for contingent workers (Row 6).
      i. If contingent labor cost saving after training exceeds unrecovered training cost, contingent workers are cost-effective.
      ii. If labor cost saving after training is less than unrecovered training cost, contingent workers are not cost-effective.

4

The Cost-Effectiveness of Contingent Labor: What Three Companies Have Found

Experience is the best teacher, and case studies report company experiences. We can theorize that contingent workers will usually cost less in compensation than core employees. We can predict that their productivity will often be a little lower. We expect that the company will usually spend some money on training them that it is unlikely to recover. But we do not know any of these things as a fact until we ask managers with experience and then analyze those experiences.

Three company case studies are the centerpiece of this chapter. The case studies are based on personal visits by the authors to the companies. In each company, several managers and supervisors were interviewed. Hard data were obtained from the company's management information system and the records of work unit managers. (However, opinions expressed by the authors do not necessarily reflect the judgment of company managers, and errors are the authors' responsibility.)

The first point of the cases is to show in concrete and graphic terms what conditions in a company lead managers to use contingent labor, how they use contingent labor, and what type of contingent workers they hire. The second point of the cases is to see if the company saves labor costs or loses money from its use of these contingent workers, and to trace the causes for the gain or loss. The third point of the cases is to show by example, using real numbers from real companies, how any manager can make similar determinations about the cost-effectiveness of contingent labor in his or her own work unit.

The cases reported in this chapter are illustrations. Case study research is not survey research. No findings from one or a few cases can ever be generalized. One company's experience will be different from another company's experience. We cannot say from these case studies that contingent labor is or is not cost-effective generally. We can say that the answer goes either way, and we can say how we get the answer.

———————————— CASE STUDY ————————————

CASE A: LOSING MONEY ON CONTINGENT LABOR IN DATA ENTRY OPERATIONS

The company is a large American commercial bank with lending operations around the world. It is successful, although like many companies in the finance industry, it is operating in turbulent times. In this case study, we look at consumer banking operations. The people in operations work mostly behind the scenes in many different offices. They process checks, credit deposits, make out account statements, move the cash in the vaults, and answer customers' questions over the telephone. We focus on one type of operating unit, which informally is called a proof center.

The bank has several proof centers, employing from 16 to 180 people each, with a total proof center employment of about 1,000 people at the time of the study. Proof centers are part of a larger Operations Division. The main job to be done is to "prove" financial balances and encode transactions for further automated processing. Most of the employees are called proof operators. They take in hundreds of thousands of checks, automated teller machine records, and vault transactions that arrive by courier every day from the bank's branches in the region. The work requires repetitive 10-key data entry from paper records, with a high demand for accuracy, until the job is done. This process is repeated every working day. It typifies the work that takes place in the "backroom" of every financial institution.

The Problem

Bank managers in proof centers have to find people to do the jobs, train them to be productive, and then try to keep them as employees. People must be on the job when you need them, and not when you don't need them—it's a matter of continuously matching labor hours supplied to labor hours demanded.

Staffing is hard to do because most of the work has to be done outside regular business hours after branches close, and because many of the jobs are repetitive. Scheduling is hard to do because it is mercilessly driven by work input that can't be controlled by the proof center manager. The amount of work to be processed depends on what the branches give to the couriers to deliver to the proof center. Whatever work comes in must be done that day because no inventory of unprocessed work is held over and no buffer stocks exist to smooth out the work flow. Every day is another deadline.

How much flexibility in labor input is required depends on how variable the workload is. How that amount of flexibility is achieved depends in part on the pattern of variation in workload over time and its predictability. For the proof centers, the workload varies unpredictably by the hour within a day—what if bad weather delays air courier deliveries or a road accident blocks bridge traffic? Work starts at midday with a workload of about 20,000 items per hour in one proof center, increases irregularly until early evening with a workload of about 150,000 items per hour, and is finished by 11 P.M. The peak load is more than seven times the lightest load. (See Figure 4-1.)

The workload also varies somewhat by the day of a week and by the week of the month. Monday is the peak day, with a workload that is 1.7 times the lightest day. (See Figure 4-2.) The proof center manager can predict daily workloads quite accurately a month in advance. The variance of actual daily workload compared to predicted was 3.7 percent in absolute terms during a recent three-week period in one proof center.

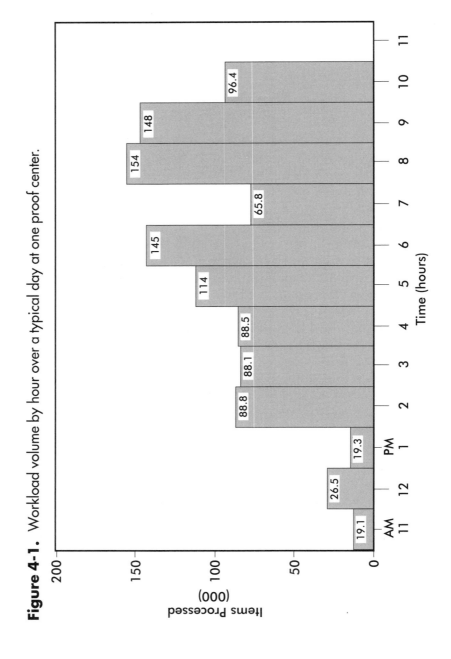

Figure 4-1. Workload volume by hour over a typical day at one proof center.

Figure 4-2. Workload volume by day over a typical week at one proof center.

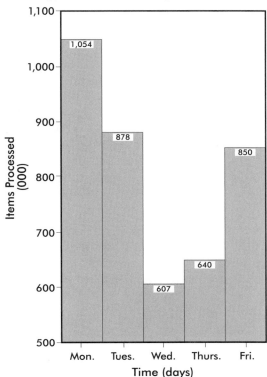

How the Company Uses Contingent Workers

To cope with changes in workload, companies can either change the number of hours worked by regular core employees or change the number of contingent employees or the hours they work. For this bank's proof centers, the extreme within-day fluctuation in workload clearly demands that part-time (part-day) employees be used. Hourly-paid part-time employees are the contingent workers. The bank has three types of employees altogether:

1. *Full-time employees,* who work at least eight hours a day, five days a week, or 40 hours a week in total. These people are core employees.

2. *Regular part-time employees*, who work an agreed schedule that is changed only infrequently. These part-timers are also core employees.
3. *Hourly part-time employees*, whose work schedules can change daily at managerial discretion. These people are contingent workers.

The Operations Division that contains the proof centers employs thousands of hourly-paid part-time workers. They account for 21 percent of the head count in consumer banking in this bank and 11 percent of full-time equivalents. They work 21 hours a week on the average. In the proof centers, hourly part-timers are used more intensively, accounting for a quarter to a third of the head count. Typical work schedules for hourly part-time proof operators look like these:

- Work Monday through Friday from 4 P.M. to 9:30 P.M., but adjust quitting time to the amount of work left to be done.
- Work two long days: Monday from 12 noon to 11 P.M. and Friday from 12 noon to 10 P.M., but leave earlier if the workload is light.

Because the workload does not vary much month by month, there is not much variation in the number of hourly part-timers over the year. Nevertheless, if there should be a gradual downturn in workload, the high turnover rate among hourly part-timers means that the size of the workforce could be quickly reduced by simply not hiring new hourly people.

The hourly workers are on the company's payroll; they are employees. They are not in-house temporaries because their jobs do not change, and they do not move around the company. The hourly part-timers do not get any benefits, but they do get a 10 percent wage premium in lieu of benefits.

Contingent Workers' Characteristics

In the consumer banking operations of this bank, contingent workers are different from full-time core employees in two main ways: (1) Contingent workers are much younger, so they tend to have a much shorter length of service with the bank; and (2) Contingent workers are all clustered in the lowest job grades and therefore earn less on the average than core employees.

Half of the bank's hourly part-time employees are age 24 or younger, and many of these people are college students. Less than 5 percent of the full-timers are this young. Half of the hourly part-timers have yet to complete one year of service with the bank, and the average total length of service is about $1^1/_2$ years. For full-timers in the consumer banking operations, 87 percent are beyond one year of service; the average is more than seven years.

Job segregation also divides contingent from core employees. Nearly 70 percent of all hourly part-timers are in one low job grade, and 97 percent are in just the four lowest job grades. In contrast, only 28 percent of the full-time employees in operations are in these same four low job grades; all the rest of them are in higher job grades. Altogether, the bank has seven nonexempt and 11 exempt job grades (the number of job grades will go down as the bank introduces broad-banding). (See Figure 4-3.)

As striking as these differences are, there is little difference in other characteristics. For example, contingent workers are not much more likely to be women than are core employees. (In this bank, as in most banks, a large majority of the workforce are women.) In one proof center, 40 percent of the proof operators are men—mostly young male college students. The education levels of contingent and core employees are scarcely any different. Hourly part-timers are more likely than full-timers to have attended some years of college rather than to have completed college, but because many of them are young and in school while they work at the bank, they probably will end up completing college proportionately as often as full-time employees. (See Table 4-1.)

Flexibility From the Core

The company also gets some workforce flexibility from its core employees. Traditional overtime hours from regular full-time employees is an accepted managerial technique. In fact, if a work unit does not use overtime, it is suspected of being overstaffed (on the other hand, units for whom overtime exceeds 5 percent of payroll are flagged for investigation for overuse of overtime). One proof center reported that

(Text continues on page 94.)

Figure 4-3. Job grades filled by full-time, core part-time (contingent) workers, operations division.

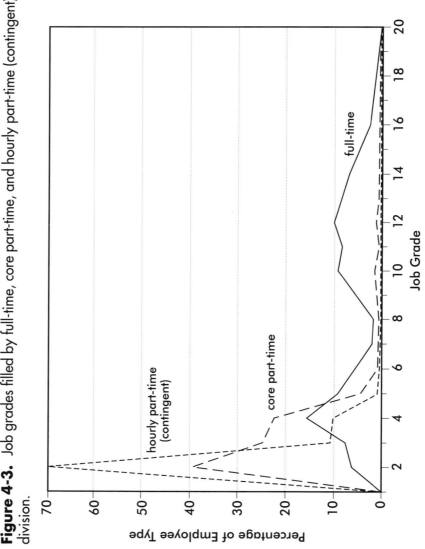

Table 4-1. Characteristics of core and contingent workers, operations division.

Characteristic	Core: Full-Time	Core: Part-Time	Contingent Hourly Part-Time
Head count (percentage of all employees)	64.0	15.4	20.6
Full-time equivalent (percentage of employees)	77.3	12.1	10.5
Average hours of work per week	43.1	28.1	18.2
Length of service (percentage distribution)			
Less than one year	13.4	13.4	49.7
1–2 years	14.7	22.5	38.7
3–5 years	12.9	13.2	7.3
More than five years	59.0	50.9	4.4
Average years of service	$\approx$7	$\approx$6	$\approx$1.5
Age (percentage distribution)			
24 and younger	4.5	14.9	49.2
25–34	32.7	28.6	23.4
35–44	35.2	26.1	12.6
45 and older	27.9	30.4	14.9
Amount of education (percentage distribution)			
High school	42.9	62.6	53.9
Some college	31.0	29.6	38.0
College graduate	26.1	7.9	8.1
Average years of school completed	13.7 yrs.	12.8 yrs.	13.0 yrs.
Average hourly earnings	$8.02	$7.06	$5.00
Gender (percentage of women)	67.1	85.6	75.3

Note: The education of many employees is unknown in the company information system, so bias in the figures is possible.
Source: Company management information system.

overtime pay accounted for 2.9 percent of its base salary expense in the first eight months of 1990.

Part-time salaried employees are also part of the core workforce (these are different people from hourly-paid contingent workers). They account for 15 percent of all consumer banking employees and 12 percent of total full-time equivalent employment. In the proof centers, the use of core part-time employees is higher: Core part-timers account for nearly 40 percent of head count and more than one-third of full-time equivalents.

A core part-time employee works a scheduled number of hours that can range from 10 to 32 hours a week as agreed at the time of employment; the average is 28 hours. Like full-time employees, salaried part-time employees can be asked to work overtime. Hours in excess of their originally-agreed schedule are called "extra time" and are paid a wage premium of 10 percent (not time-and-a-half) even if the total number of hours worked is less than eight in a day or 40 in a week. However, most managers are reluctant to go to "extra time" for core part-time employees, preferring instead to get more labor hours in a day from hourly part-time contingent workers.

Measuring Cost-Effectiveness

The bank's proof centers use contingent workers to match their workforce to their fluctuating workload. Is this use of contingent labor cost-effective? Is it an economical or an expensive solution to the fluctuating workload problem?

Cost-effectiveness depends on wages and benefits, productivity, training and other fixed costs of employment, and time on the job. We want to compare these variables for contingent workers with core employees, following the methods outlined in Chapter 3.

Wages and Benefits

There is no surprise here: Core employees get more compensation than contingent employees. Full-time proof operators get a salary of $14,700 per year (about $7.07 per hour), and benefits valued by the company at 27.3 percent of base pay. Their total compensation is $9.00 an hour. Core part-time employees receive the same pay and benefits as full-time employees, most of which are prorated to their hours worked.

Hourly part-time proof operators are hired at $6.25 an hour and get a raise to $7.77 once they complete their training and reach the required minimum output rate; nine months are allowed to reach this rate. This post-training wage is set to match the full-time rate of pay plus a 10 percent wage premium added in lieu of benefits, which are not paid. Therefore hourly part-timers actually earn 71¢ per hour more in straight wages than their full-time counterparts, but their total compensation cost to the company is $1.23 an hour less.

All employees can earn incentive pay in addition to base pay if their output rate exceeds 1,300 items per hour and quality levels are maintained. Among all proof operators, about 80 percent get incentive pay, amounting to about 70¢ per hour.

Productivity

Managers in the bank believe that the productivity of hourly part-time and full-time employees is about the same. In principle, part-timers might do better because repetitive jobs, as many operations jobs are, can be done faster for shorter periods of time. On the other hand, contingent workers may be less committed to their jobs—if commitment matters to productivity for these types of jobs.

Productivity is measured in the bank by quantity of output produced and by supervisors' performance appraisals, which include aspects of performance such as quality of output, attendance, and subjective features. According to actual company data, the performance appraisals of operations employees overall show that contingent workers have the lowest performance, with an average rating of 3.3 (where 5 is best), compared to 3.8 for full-time employees and 3.6 for core part-time employees. For proof operators in particular, the productivity story looks similar, although the evidence is not thorough enough to be sure. In terms of both performance appraisals and output rates, contingent part-time workers turn in results that are roughly one-tenth to one-third below core part-time employees, who are the best comparison group. But in one proof center, contingent workers had better productivity results than full-time core employees. (See Table 4-2 for details and explanations.)

Table 4-2. Productivity of core and contingent workers.

Productivity Measure	Core: Full-Time	Core: Part-Time	Contingent: Hourly Part-Time
Performance Appraisal			
Operations Divison	3.8	3.6	3.3
Proof Center A	4.7	4.0	3.0
Proof Center B	Met	Exceeds	Met/Exceeds
Output Rate			
Proof Center A	1,834	2,030	1,272
Proof Center B	1,200–1,300	1,500–1,650	1,400–1,500

Notes: Performance appraisals for the Operations Division include all employees in this division. A score of 5 is best, and 1 is worst. Appraisals are unavailable for 38 percent of the contingent workers in the Operations Division because, in most cases, their length of service is not long enough. Appraisals are missing for 12 percent of full-time and 10 percent of core part-time employees in this division. Performance appraisals for the proof centers apply to proof operators only. In Proof Center A, the data refer to the top six people only; among contingent workers in this proof center, some have a length of time on the job that is shorter than the length of the training period, and thus the output rate for contingent workers is probably understated (performance appraisal data for this proof center exclude these short-service people). In Proof Center B, "Met" = 3 and "Exceeds" = 4.
Source: Company management information system and proof center managers.

Unit Labor Cost

If we balance the lower compensation cost for contingent workers against their probable lower productivity, we can find out whether their unit labor cost is higher or lower than for core employees. Because the productivity data are not conclusive, we adopt alternative scenarios to illustrate a range of outcomes.

The most conservative scenario that compares contingent to core part-time workers is from Proof Center B: The output rate of contingent part-time workers is about 7.9 percent less than the output rate of core part-time workers. This productivity shortfall is less than the 13.7 percent saving in their compensation. Therefore, the unit labor cost of production for contingent workers is lower than for core part-timers in this work unit. (In the same proof center, the contingent workers show a higher rate of output than core full-time workers, so the combination of higher productivity and lower compensation clearly means lower unit labor cost for contingent workers than for full-time core workers—about 30 percent lower—in this proof center.) But in Proof Center A, both the performance appraisal and productivity results for contingent workers fall far below the results for core employees (by 11 to 23 percent). This shortfall outweighs the lower compensation paid to contingent workers so that their unit labor cost is higher.

Training

Training is required for every new proof operator. It begins with formal training of roughly 200 hours of the work time of the trainee spread over about three months (for hourly part-time employees) and uses the time of a full-time trainer. At the end of three months of formal training, the proof operator must produce 800 items per hour to continue employment. By the end of nine months, the operator's output rate must increase with experience to a rate of 1,200 items per hour—if this rate is not achieved after nine months (this is the time managers expect it takes to climb the learning curve), the operator loses his or her job. The cost of training consists of (1) the direct cost of the trainer's pay, plus equipment and space dedicated to training, and (2) the opportunity cost of the trainee's wage less the value of usable output produced by the trainee during the training period. This cost can be recovered by the company if trained workers produce value of output that exceeds their compensation for a long enough period of time after training is completed.

Taken together, these two training costs are estimated to run about $910 to $970 per trainee for hourly part-time employees. Actually, $1,030 to $1,090 is incurred for the initial three-month period, but during the on-the-job training period from four to nine months the trainees' value of output produced actually exceeds the compensation they are paid. (See the Appendix to this case for the calculations.)

How long does it take to recover the training costs? One proof center manager said it takes a year. Our calculations bear this out for contingent employees. Of course, the training payback period depends on the productivity of the trained employee. If we assume an output rate of 1,400 items per hour (an optimistic figure), the payback period is just about one year. When we add the length of the training period itself, the calendar length of service required for the company to recover its training cost is about 20 months for hourly part-time employees.

Turnover

One of the most notable and disconcerting features of contingent employees for this bank is its exceedingly high turnover rates. Among all hourly part-timers in operations, the average length of service is only about $1^1/_2$ years, which implies an annual turnover rate of 67 percent. In the first proof center mentioned, the length of service among hourly proof operators is still less—14 months. In the other proof center studied, the average hourly-paid proof operator stays only 6.2 months. This is a turnover rate of nearly 200 percent.

High turnover among people in bank service jobs is endemic. These jobs are not exciting career-track jobs. But in addition, most of the hourly proof operators at this bank are young and many are students; these people will move on when their studies are completed, no matter what the job is like that they now hold. High turnover need not be a problem for the bank if it is easy to find replacements who can be productive immediately. Unfortunately, that is not the case for proof operators because training is necessary and costly.

The Result

The analysis shows that on average, training costs for contingent workers are not recovered. Hourly part-time workers stay with a proof center for as much as 14 months, but the training cost recovery time is 20 months. Therefore, training is an extra cost of employment for contingent workers, above and beyond their wages. The amount of this extra cost of unrecovered training is $540 (see the Appendix to this case for the calculations). Training is not an investment with a positive return; it is just another cost of doing business that contingent workers bring. To enable the company to break even on the money it spends on training contingent workers, either an output rate higher than that which is actually achieved at either proof center studied, or a length of service that is longer than currently achieved, would have to prevail. (In contrast to contingent workers, core employees appear to pay back their training cost, given their actual length of service, assuming conservatively that their productivity is equal to that of contingent workers.)

Does the extra cost of training make contingent workers more expensive to use than core employees? Of course they are more expensive if they already have higher unit labor cost, as seems to be true in one of the proof centers. But what about the proof center where contingent workers seem to have lower unit labor cost? Does the unrecovered training cost there outweigh the lower unit labor cost advantage that contingent workers have?

The answer, conservatively figured, is yes. Contingent workers are not cost-effective in the proof centers of this bank. If the unrecovered training cost is spread over the working time of contingent workers after their training is completed until they quit the company, it is as if they were paid an extra $1.32 an hour (see the Appendix for the calculations)—that is, as though their pay were $9.09 an hour (not $7.77), which is above the core workers' compensation of $9.00 an hour. Paying more but getting less is not cost-effective.

This finding does not mean that contingent workers should not be used. It means that they are high-cost as currently used, and that high cost may be unavoidable. The dramatic fluctuations in workload have to be managed somehow, and some type of part-time staffing and scheduling is necessary.

Summary

Proof centers in this bank use hourly part-time employees as contingent workers to achieve the flexibility required to quickly adjust the size of the workforce to the dramatically fluctuating size of the workload. These contingent employees get higher pay than core employees in the same jobs but no benefits; their total compensation package is less. Their productivity is less than core employees in most comparisons but not all; their unit labor cost is higher in some instances and lower in others. Training costs about $940 for each new contingent worker, and this cost is not fully recovered by the company. By conservative figuring, contingent workers in proof centers are not cost-effective. They are an expensive solution to the flexibility problem.

———————————— CASE STUDY ————————————

CASE B: MAKING MONEY ON CONTINGENT LABOR IN DATA ENTRY OPERATIONS

The company in Case B is different from the company in Case A, but the work is the same: data entry in the backroom operations of a commercial bank. The Case B bank has business around the world, just like the bank in Case A. It also has gone through difficult times, but was stable with a promising future when this case study was done.

The Problem

The problem faced by managers is a familiar one: how to rapidly adjust the amount of labor on the job to cope with big fluctuations in the amount of work to be done. The workload in the backroom operations varies mainly according to the week of the month (some fluctuation exists by day of the week as in Case A). The first two weeks are heavy, and the rest of the month is lighter. The work unit we examined, called lockbox operations, operates around the clock in three shifts.

How the Company Uses Contingent Workers

To get the numerical flexibility to cope with the fluctuating need for labor, the company uses temporary workers supplied by staffing companies. The temporaries come to work during the first week or two of the month and work full days (or full shifts). Some of them are not needed later in the month, but they return for the first week or two of the next month. Regular full-time employees also do these backroom jobs. However, temporaries outnumber regular employees during the peak periods. In the course of the month overall, the company gets more hours of work from temporaries than it does from its own employees.

This bank uses temporaries from an agency as its contingent workers not only because the intermittent full-shift work schedule suits temporaries, but also because, managers believe, temporaries are more cost-effective than core full-time employees. In this labor market at the time of the study, the supply of people who are willing to work this type of schedule is ample.

Measuring Cost-Effectiveness

Managers in lockbox operations have good information on all the components of cost-effectiveness—wages, benefits, and agency fees; productivity; training costs; and time on the job. We analyze each of these components in turn.

Wages, Benefits, and Agency Fees

According to 1992 statistics, most of the regular employees serving as data entry operators receive an annual salary that hovers around $14,500. This figure refers to people with experience in the job grade for data entry operators (the salary range for this job grade is $12,850 to $19,270). Because most regular employees have been temporary workers in these jobs previously, they earn more than the entry-level wage for their job grade. They receive benefits that amount to 27 percent of salary on the average. The workweek at the time of the study was 35 hours (subsequently it was increased to 40 hours). Total compensation for regular employees is $10.12 per hour (Table 4-3).

Temporary workers usually begin at an hourly wage rate of $7, although a few start at $6.50. The agencies that supply them are paid

Table 4-3. Cost of wages and benefits for regular employees and temporary workers.

	Regular Employee	Temporary Worker
Wage	$14,500/year = $7.97/hour	$7 per hour = $12,740/year
Benefits @ 27%	$3,915/year = $2.15/hour	None
Agency fee @ 27%	None	$1.88 per hour
Total compensation	$18,415/year = $10.12/hour	$8.88 per hour = $16,162/year

Note: The annual wage figure for regular employees applies to the job grade for data entry operators; these employees have been temporary workers previously, so this annual wage is above the starting salary for this grade, $12,850. Raises are given after one year, based on performance, and average about 5.5 percent.

For temporary workers, $7 is the typical starting wage rate, although occasionally some temporaries start at $6.50 per hour. Raises of 25¢ to 50¢ per hour (which is 3.5 percent to 7 percent) are sometimes awarded to temporary workers for good performance, and raises of $1 (roughly 14 percent) may be awarded for exceptional performance.

The workweek up to April 1, 1992, was 35 hours (5 days of 7 hours), which is 1,820 hours per year. After April 1, 1992, the workweek was lengthened to 40 hours per week.

a fee that averages about 27 percent of their hourly wage. Temporary workers do not receive benefits from the company, although some may be eligible for them through their agencies. The total cost to the company for temporary workers is $8.88 per hour. Pay raises of 25¢ to 50¢ per hour are awarded to some temporary workers for good performance, and raises of as much as $1 are occasionally offered for exceptional performance.

The wage and agency fee cost to the company for temporary workers is less than the wage and benefit cost of regular employees by $1.24 per hour or 12.2 percent. This difference is due solely to the lower wage paid to temporary workers; agency fees for temporaries are the same as benefit costs for regular employees.

Productivity

Labor productivity is determined by the quantity and quality of output that workers produce. In the backroom operations of this bank, quantity is measured by physical pieces of output produced per hour, and quality can be measured by error rate as reported by customers. To correctly assess productivity differences, we look at temporary and regular employees who do the same job at the same place and who have the same supervisor. We measure output rates for each of four types of data entry work and two types of mail opening work. Output rates for data entry operators are automatically measured by the equipment that the operators use, and the company routinely uses these data to flag poor performers. These are nonintrusive measures.

Whether a worker is contingent or core, or temporary or regular, is not the only factor that affects his or her productivity. Differences in how the company uses temporary and regular employees can also affect productivity. In this work unit, temporaries work irregular schedules and put in fewer hours than regular employees, and they are more likely to work on the first or third shifts than on the second shift. In this work unit, both amount of experience on the job and shift worked affect productivity. We account for these factors when we analyze the productivity of contingent versus core workers.

The personal characteristics of temporary workers—such as age, gender, education, and family status—may differ from those of regular employees. These personal differences, if they exist, might also cause productivity differences. But these characteristics belong to the workers themselves, and most cannot be changed by company managers who hire temporaries. Therefore we do not seek to control for these characteristics.

The company's own data lead to a clear conclusion: The productivity of temporary workers is lower than the productivity of regular employees. Both temporary data entry operators and temporary mail openers produce less output per hour than regular employees doing the same jobs. The difference is about 7 percent as a weighted average. Aside from lower output, temporary data entry operators have a higher error rate than regular employees, although for both groups the error rate is so small that company managers are not concerned about it. (See Table 4-4.)

Table 4-4. Productivity of regular vs. temporary workers, lockbox operations.

Productivity Measure	Regular Output/Hour	Temporary Output/Hour	% Difference for Temporaries
Data Entry Productivity			
Product C	1,374	1,274	−7.3
Product R	1,090	1,002	−8.1
Product M	708	702	−0.8
Product W	319	305	−4.4
Mail Opening Productivity			
Product H	1,202	1,120	−6.8
Product L	756	693	−8.3
Data Entry Error Rate			
Errors per 10,000 items	0.40	0.54	−35.0

Notes: Products C, R, M, and W are different types of data entry jobs, and Products H and L are different types of mail opening jobs with varying degrees of difficulty and output rate expectations. The output figures are monthly averages of individual productivity of 32 regular and 85 temporary workers from August 1991 through January 1992. The number of observations per cell in the table ranges from 85 to 191. Productivity differences for Products C, R, H, and L are statistically significant at the 99 percent level of confidence, according to an analysis of variance in which shift worked and number of hours worked per month are covariates with employment status; Product W productivity difference is significant at the 90 percent level; Product M difference is not statistically significant. The volume-weighted average productivity difference for all products is about 7 percent.
Source: Tabulated from company management information systems.

The temporary workers in lockbox operations have less experience in this company and on a given job than the regular employees. At any point in time, some of this work unit's temporaries have several months of experience on the job while others are quite new, with only a few weeks of experience. If we divide all the temporary workers into two groups—less-experienced and more-experienced—we find that the less-experienced have lower productivity than the more-experienced. (A "new" temporary becomes an "experienced" temporary after one or two months when the company gives the worker an identification number for its information system.) New temporaries produce about 8 percent less than regular employees, while the more experienced ones only fall $2^1/_2$ percent short. In this company, lack of job experience is an important reason why temporary workers have lower productivity than regular employees.

Unit Labor Cost

The unit cost of labor—compensation cost of labor per unit of output produced—depends on both productivity and wages. For data entry operations in this work unit, the 7 percent productivity disadvantage of temporary workers is more than offset by their 12 percent compensation cost advantage to the company. Therefore, the unit labor cost of temporary workers is less than the unit labor cost of regular employees by about 5 percent.

Training Costs

The company hires temporary workers who already have keyboard skills—this requirement is made known to the agencies that supply the temporaries. However, some initial training is still needed to acquaint the new temporaries with the company's jobs, machines, and work flow.

The initial training that is provided by the company is all on-the-job training that occurs in two stages. During the new temporary worker's first three days on the job, an experienced data entry operator spends time with the new worker. For the rest of about four weeks, the new worker is expected to improve speed and accuracy without assistance from a trainer until the threshold output level of 1,300 items per hour (for clean retail data entry) is achieved.

The cost of on-the-job training to the company arises from two sources. One is the output lost from supervisors who spend time training the new temporary workers instead of producing output themselves. The other is the wages paid to trainees that exceed the value of output they produce during the training period.

The cost of lost output from supervisors is estimated to be $112. The net cost of wages and agency fees that exceed the value of output produced by the temporary worker during the four-week training period is estimated to be $150. Thus, the total training cost is $262 per new temporary worker. (See the Appendix to this case.)

The cost of training is quite small because there is no formal classroom training and the on-the-job training period is very short, which in turn follows from the company's practice of hiring temporaries who already have keyboard skills.

The fact that new temporary workers are paid less than regular employees doing the same work means that if they produce output at the expected rate of 1,300 items per hour, their production has higher value to the company ($10.12) than the payments the company makes to them ($8.88). The crossover point when the value of a new temporary worker's output exceeds the wages and fees the company pays comes even before on-the-job training is completed—in the fourteenth day of service. At this juncture, the new temporary worker's output is only 1,147 items per hour, according to our model.

In the company's experience, the actual average output rate achieved by temporary workers is 1,274 items per hour, which is worth $9.91 to the company, but the cost to the company is only $8.88 per hour. This means that the training cost is paid back at the rate of $1.03 per hour. The total training cost of $262 can be recovered by the company in 254 working hours, which is about 10 weeks of calendar time. Thus, four weeks of training plus 10 weeks of training cost recovery time amounts to a total length of service of 14 weeks or about 3$^{1}/_{2}$ months that is required for the company to break even on its training investment in temporary workers. (See the Appendix to this case for the calculations.) The actual average length of service of temporary employees is longer than this, perhaps about seven months. This means that the cost the company incurs to train new temporary workers is repaid in the form of value of output they produce that exceeds the wages they are paid during their average time on the job with the company.

If a temporary worker is given a pay raise of 50¢ an hour after training is completed because that worker is achieving an output rate of 1,300 items per hour (more than the temporary worker average of 1,274 items per hour), then the payback of training costs occurs at a slower rate, and the training cost payback period is lengthened. But calculations show that this payback time is still shorter than the average temporary's time on the job, and so all training costs are recovered by the company. (The numbers are that the training cost payback rate is 59¢ an hour, and the paycheck period is a little more than five months.)

The Result

This company is saving money by its use of contingent workers in lockbox operations. The small cost incurred by the company to train new temporary workers is fully recovered. In addition, these workers have lower unit labor cost than regular employees doing the same jobs. Therefore, contingent labor is clearly cost-effective in this company.

Summary

Lockbox operations in this bank use temporary workers supplied by agencies in order to quickly match the amount of labor time available to the workloads that fluctuate according to the week of the month. The temporaries get lower pay than regular employees doing the same jobs. The fees paid to the agencies are the same as the benefits paid to regular employees, so labor compensation is lower for contingent workers. The productivity of the temporaries is lower, much of which is explained by their shorter time on the job. However, the shortfall in temporaries' productivity is less than the compensation saving, so the unit labor cost of temporaries is lower. Training costs for new temporary workers are low mainly because the agencies are able to supply workers who are already trained. All of the training costs are recovered by the company. Contingent workers are cost-effective in lockbox operations in this bank. However, company managers believe this result would not transfer to other work settings, where skill requirements are higher and training needs greater, or to other labor markets.

———————————— **CASE STUDY** ————————————

CASE C: HIGH COSTS FOR CONTINGENT LABOR IN HIGH-TECH ASSEMBLY

The company in Case C is a contrast to the banks in Cases A and B. The Case C company is a high-tech manufacturing corporation, one of whose main divisions makes industrial controls. The products are electronic devices that automatically regulate production processes in diverse applications ranging from oil refineries to food processing plants. At the factory that we study, about two-thirds of the employees are production workers who build products such as circuit boards, or who in turn assemble these products into complete automated control systems that are unique to each customer. The remaining one-third of the employees are scientists, customer service people, and managers.

The work is done in teams; no one is a solo player. Production operations are carried out by about 40 work units comprising about 20 people each who are jointly responsible for getting the product out.

The Problem

The reasons for using contingent labor in Company C have little to do with fluctuating workloads, unlike Companies A and B, although there was some uneven bunching of customer contracts years ago. Instead, the company's contingent labor story began with a traumatic historical event. A succession of 13 major layoffs occurred between 1978 and 1984, and that turned out to be a painful experience for the company, which had never before known such adversity. This bad experience resulted in a vow to protect employment in the future against downturns in the company's business. This is a case of building a buffer of contingent workers around a core of regular employees to protect the latter's jobs.

This is also a case of managerial belief that contingent labor is cheaper than core labor. Since these workers were thought to be cheaper, large numbers were brought in, more than necessary for a buffer against cyclical downturns.

But now, company managers are having second thoughts. In an

ever more competitive global business environment, can high output and high quality be achieved with large numbers of contingent workers? Are these people really helping to reduce labor costs? Why, some managers ask, do we need so many contingent workers? In the 1980s, the company's demand for labor varied not only with cycles of boom and bust in the industry, but also with ups and downs in customer orders and delivery dates from week to week and month to month within a year. Customers were concentrated in one or two industries such as oil and gas refining. But now the customer base is diversified across several industries so that the order flow is more even than it was and the need for numerical flexibility is diminished. A fluctuating workload is just not a factor that motivates the use of contingent labor.

Still, other managers point out the ease of dealing with contingent workers. For example, if a temporary worker from an agency is not performing well, he or she can simply be sent back and another one obtained.

How the Company Uses Contingent Workers

This is a classic case of the birth of a core-ring strategy. The company wanted numerical flexibility—it wanted to be able to change the number of people at work as the need for labor input changed over time.

The contingent workers are temporary workers obtained from agencies. They are expected to work at the company on one job for nine months, extendable to 12 months. Temporaries are not supposed to stay longer than one year by company policy in order to avoid the appearance of an employment relationship. In fact, nearly 70 percent of the temporaries stay less than nine months. Of the company's total current staff of about 800 people, more than 200 are agency temporaries. The other 600 are regular salaried employees. The temporaries as a group are younger than the core employees, and they are more likely to be men (see Table 4-5).

Measuring Cost-Effectiveness

Wages, Benefits, and Agency Fees

A major reason for the use of contingent labor, aside from buffering the jobs of core employees, is that many company managers believe

Table 4-5. Characteristics of core and contingent workers in assembly jobs.

Characteristic	Core	Contingent
Age: Percentage who are:		
24 and under	11%	22%
25–34	26	38
35–44	28	26
45–54	24	10
55 and over	12	4
Gender: Percentage who are women	61	41
Job grade: Percentage who are in:		
Grade 1 (entry-level grade)	57	100
Grade 2	34	0
Grades 3, 4, 5, 6	9	0
Wages for entry-level assembler:		
Hourly wage rate	$6.92	$6.00
Benefits @ 28.5%	$1.97	0
Agency fee @ 24%	0	$1.44
Total hourly cost to company	$8.89	$7.44

Note: Hourly wage rate for entry-level assembler who is a core employee is calculated from the salary schedule of $1,200 per month ($14,400 per year); core employees are salaried, not hourly paid, even though they are in nonexempt jobs.
Source: Tabulated from company management information system.

that the use of contingent labor reduces labor costs. They believe this because temporaries are paid lower wages than regular company employees who are in the same job grade ($6.00 an hour compared to $6.92 in the entry-level job grade), and because they do not receive fringe benefits. Compensation for regular employees is $8.89 an hour, but for contingent workers it is $7.44, including agency fees.

Productivity

Ten years later and with a new management in place, questions are being raised about the productivity of contingent labor. In 1990, the company adopted a business goal of achieving world-class manufacturing standards. The goal involves reducing unit cost of production and increasing customer service to match the best results obtained by any company worldwide. The specific methods to reach the goal are to reduce product defects, inventories, and order-to-shipment time.

The question is: Do contingent workers contribute to the company's world-class manufacturing goal, or does contingent labor make it more difficult to achieve this goal? Because all the work is done in teams, no individual productivity measurements are taken, and no individual performance appraisals are done. Instead, the issue under debate is the effect of contingent labor on the functioning of work teams, which many managers believe to be adverse. How can work teams function optimally, they ask, if temporary workers are continually coming and going?

Training

Training is a high cost of doing business in this company. All new workers, including contingent workers, must be trained quite extensively before they can be fully productive. High technology and team-based operations mean high training, even for production jobs.

The company provides three types of training to its workers: First, all new workers receive initial classroom introduction in job skills as well as an orientation to the workplace. Second, all new workers receive on-the-job training at their work site. Third, all workers get continuing classroom coursework periodically throughout the year.

Because contingent workers are not permitted to work at the company for more than one year, training must be provided to new contingent workers each year. No new core employees are hired; instead, any need for new core employees is filled from the ranks of contingent workers.

Every new worker gets initial classroom instruction conducted by company trainers on-site. This consists of skills training as well as orientation to the job and work site. The course length is five days for standard products assemblers, three days for systems assemblers, and three days for nonassembly workers.

This training costs a total of $478 for each new contingent worker. Of this amount, $176 pays for the trainer's compensation, $74 goes for the facility plus $10 in consumable materials for each trainee, and $218 is the amount of wages paid to the trainee during this time when he or she is not producing any output. (For details on how this figure and the other training figures to follow were calculated, see the Appendix to this case. Figure 4-4 displays this and other training costs graphically.)

The company provides on-the-job training during the first six to eight weeks of work time after initial classroom instruction for new assembly workers. A certified experienced assembler works with a new worker at the work site, with decreasing intensity as the trainee's productivity increases. The company loses output from these supervisors during the training period. At the same time, the worker is paid a wage but does not produce output of equal value, so this is a second source of cost.

The cost of on-the-job training for each new temporary assembly worker totals $1,206. This cost is built up from $803 in lost output from the supervisor, plus $403 in trainee's wages that exceed the value of the output that he or she produces during this period.

The company provides continuing coursework to work teams as a group on a variety of topics ranging from manufacturing processes to teamwork skills. This training is conducted by company personnel on-site throughout the year. Contingent workers take these courses along with regular employees.

The cost of continuing classroom training totals $419 per contingent worker per year. Of this total, $52 is incurred from trainers' compensation, $10 is consumable materials, $30 is facilities cost per trainee, and $327 is the wages paid to the worker during this period when no output is being produced.

The total cost of initial classroom instruction, on-the-job training, and continuing coursework for a contingent worker for a year is a very high $2,183 (see Table 4-6 for a summary). The largest of these components is on-the-job training. This cost is quite high because both supervisor and trainee are being paid for one-on-one training for many days, but neither is producing full rates of output. (If core employees were hired directly from the external labor market, the cost of training them in their first year of service would be about $2,552—a higher figure because they are paid higher wages.)

New contingent workers are supplied by temporary employment agencies, so there is little or none of the usual hiring cost. However, the company interviews prospective contingent workers who are sent by the agencies. Both the work unit manager and employees interview candidates, from which a selection is made. Interviewing

Figure 4-4. What the company pays out and gets back for new contingent workers who receive training—electronic assembly.

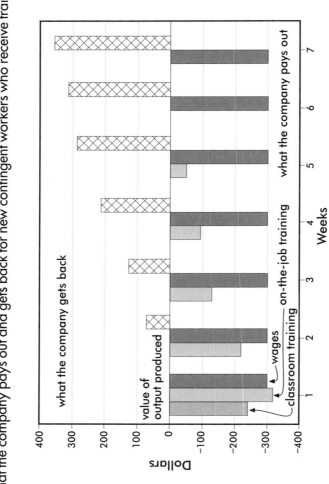

Notes: Classroom training occurs in the first week; the cost is the trainer's salary, space rental, and materials. On-the-job training takes place in the first five weeks with decreasing intensity; the cost is the supervisor's lost output. Wages are paid to the contingent worker-trainee at regular rates throughout the training period. The contingent worker-trainee begins to produce output in the second week and increases productivity steadily. In the sixth week the trained worker first produces value of output that exceeds wages paid.

Table 4-6. Costs of training and selecting contingent workers in electronics assembly jobs.

Type of Cost	Contingent	Core
Initial classroom training	$ 478	$ 521
On-the-job training	1,206	1,548
Continuing training	419	483
Selection interviewing	80	80
Total	$2,183	$2,632

Source: Company data and estimates by the authors.

takes time away from production. We calculate this foregone output cost to be $80 per new contingent worker.

Suppose that the compensation of core employees in entry-level assembler jobs, which is $17,780 per year or $8.89 per hour, is equal to the value of the output they produce. (The principle that wages equal the value of additional output produced is widely used in labor economics, and will be more or less true on the average if labor markets are working efficiently and freely.) The payment made by the company for contingent workers is $7.44 per hour, which is $1.45 per hour less than the value of output they produce once fully trained, if they are equally as productive as core employees. Then $1.45 per hour is the rate at which the training investment in contingent labor is repaid. The amount of the combined training and selection investment is $2,183 per contingent worker; this is how much the company has to recover.

The payback period for the company to recover its training and selection investment in contingent labor is 1,505 hours, which is more than nine months (about 39 weeks). Add to this the length of training itself (about seven weeks including up to five days of initial classroom training plus six weeks or more of on-the-job training). Therefore, the training cost recovery period that starts when training ends requires a total length of service of 46 weeks or about 10½ months.

The expected employment period for contingent workers is nine months. The company is not able to recover its training and selection investment in this time period. Only if contingent workers stay on the job beyond the length of time the company expects of them can training costs be recovered. In actual fact, the length of service of contingent workers is on average much less than nine months. Two-thirds stay less; the average time on the job is about seven months. Training costs are not recovered.

(In some cases, contingent workers are given a 50¢ an hour merit pay increase after six months; while this pay increase would appear to reduce the rate at which the company recovers its training investment, we assume that the pay increase reflects a corresponding productivity increase so that the training payback period is unaffected.)

The Result

Training and selection costs for contingent workers that are unrecovered are an extra expense incurred for the use of this type of labor. The unrecovered training cost is about $908 per worker. Losing $908 per worker on training is like paying each one of them an extra dollar an hour in wages for every hour worked after training is completed (see the Appendix to this case for details). However, this is still less than core employees' compensation. But the gap becomes quite narrow.

In the final analysis, whether contingent workers are cheaper than core employees depends on their productivity. This is precisely the issue now being questioned by company managers.

So far we have just assumed that the productivity of contingent workers is equal to the productivity of core employees. But company managers now begin to doubt it. No one knows for certain because there is no absolute quantitative measure of individual productivity in a teamwork environment. There is understandably no systematic performance appraisal system for temporary workers.

On the one hand, contingent workers might contribute as much as core employees. Remember, a temporary worker who does not measure up is quickly sent back to the agency that supplied him or her. In addition, since occasionally contingent workers are hired on as regular core employees, there is an incentive for some of them to perform well if they have this goal in mind.

The critical question is whether contingent workers can function effectively as members of teams, which is how work is done in this factory. What makes a production worker a good teamwork contributor? Aside from individual quantity and quality of output produced, the contributing worker needs to be able to integrate into the work team. This means the worker must understand the work processes throughout the unit, be aware of the habits of other team members, possess a sense of the larger work environment, and feel a stake in the success of the team and the company. Can all of this knowledge and commitment be found in contingent workers who expect from their first day on the job that they will be gone in several months or a year? Can teams be smoothly functioning production units when one of their members changes every month or two? As global competition raises the stakes for higher quality and faster order-to-shipment times, company managers suspect the answers to these questions are no.

So, yes, maybe contingent workers are a little cheaper in terms of tangible employment costs (their low wages compensate for their high training costs). But, no, maybe the unmeasured damage they do to team-based production means that their lower cost does not compensate for their overall performance. In this company, the "contingent workers are cheaper" belief is fading from view as the white light of work unit performance grows stronger.

Summary

Contingent workers are temporaries from help supply services in this factory that assembles electronic components. Their use started more than ten years ago in order to build a buffer to protect the jobs of regular employees, and because they were thought to be cheaper. In fact, the wages and agency fees for the temporaries are less than the wages and benefits for regular employees. However, the company's adoption of world-class manufacturing goals has raised the question of the effect of contingent workers on work unit performance. Training costs in this high-tech industry are high, and not all of them are recovered before the temporary workers leave the company. Contingent workers are not as cheap as they seem to be. On the other hand, the added expense of unrecovered training costs still is not enough to compensate for the considerable wage gap between contingent and core workers. Whether or not contingent workers are cost-effective depends finally on their contribution to the team-based production methods of this factory. To sum up, company managers fear that the short length of job service of temporary workers impedes the company's efforts to improve quality, reduce inventory, and shorten order-to-shipment times for customers. Cost-effectiveness is in doubt.

Putting the Cases Together: What to Expect for Cost-Effectiveness

Experiences from the three companies discussed in this chapter relate stories about the cost-effectiveness of contingent labor. Each story is different, but put together, some strong findings emerge. If we synthesize these experiences across the three cases, what might we expect about the cost-effectiveness of contingent labor?

The main variables to measure to determine cost-effectiveness are compensation (wages and benefits or agency fee), productivity, training and other fixed employment costs, and time on the job.

Lower Compensation and Lower Productivity

Contingent workers are paid less than regular employees doing the same jobs in these companies. The temporary workers in Companies B and C get a smaller hourly wage rate, and the fee the companies pay to the agency that supplies them is about the same as the benefit rate for regular employees. The part-time contingent workers in Company A get no benefits and their 10 percent wage premium is much lower than benefits would be. (See Table 4-7 for a summary of these and other key case study data.)

In all of these cases, the supply of people available for contingent work is ample, even if contingent work is not their preferred choice of a work life or style. The labor markets where these companies are located had average unemployment rates. If the labor markets were tighter, the compensation story might very well turn around.

In these three cases, contingent workers do jobs—data entry and product assembly—that are common among temporary and hourly part-time workers. These are not highly specialized professional jobs like some other temporaries or contract workers do, so the findings from these cases may not apply to that type of work. Remember that case studies cannot be generalized, and your experiences may differ

Table 4-7. Summary of cost-effectiveness of contingent labor at work units in three companies.

Variable	Company A: Bank Proof Center	Company B: Bank Lockbox Operation	Company C: Electronics Assembly
Type of job	Data entry	Data entry	Electronics assembly
Contingent workers	Hourly part-time employees	Part-time agency temporaries	Full-time agency temporaries
Wage rate			
core:	$7.07/hour + incentive	$7.97/hour	$6.92/hour
contingent:	$6.25 per hour raised to $7.77 after training + incentive	$7.00/hour raised to $7.25 to $7.75 based on merit	$6.00/hour raised to $6.50 based on merit
Benefits			
core:	27.3% of base wage = $1.93/hour	27% of base wage = $2.15/hour	28.5% of base wage = $1.97/hour
contingent:	None for contingents but 10% wage premium paid instead	None for contingents unless provided by agency	None for contingents unless provided by agency
Agency fee	not applicable	27% of hourly wage	24% of hourly wage
Total labor cost			
core:	$9.00/hour	$10.12/hour	$8.89/hour
contingent:	$7.77/hour—13.7% or $1.23 less than core	$8.88/hour—12% or $1.24 less than core	$7.44/hour—16% or $1.45 less than core
Productivity	Contingent less than core part-time by 1/10 to 1/3 but results mixed; 7.9% less in 1 unit	Contingent less than core by 7% controling for shift and hours	Individual productivity not appraised; teamwork performance may be hampered by contingents

(continues)

Table 4-7. (Continued).

Variable	Company A: Bank Proof Center	Company B: Bank Lockbox Operation	Company C: Electronics Assembly
Unit labor cost	Higher for contingents in some cases; lower by 5.8% in 1 unit	Lower for contingents by 5% in 1 unit	Lower for contingents by 16% *if* productivity is equal, but this is doubtful
Training cost for contingents	$910 to $970 per new contingent worker (200 hours of classroom and 6 months of on-the-job)	$260 per new contingent worker (4 weeks of on-the-job training)	$2,183 per new contingent worker ($3\frac{2}{3}$ days of classroom, 6 weeks of on-the-job, $5\frac{1}{2}$ days of continuing)
Training payback	About 20 months	About 4 to 6 months	Nearly 12 months
Average length of service	14 months in 1 unit	7 months in 1 unit	7 months; 12 months is maximum
Is training cost recovered?	No	Yes	No
Is contingent labor cost-effective?	No—unit labor cost probably higher, but even if unit labor cost is lower, unrecovered training cost exceeds unit labor cost saving	Yes—unit labor cost is lower and training cost is recovered	Depends—if productivity were equal, savings from lower unit labor cost would exceed unrecovered training cost; but performance from contingents is probably lower

from these if your labor market and management practices differ from these companies.

Productivity of contingent workers is also lower in these companies. Measured output rates for these individuals are lower and performance appraisal ratings, when done, are lower (though there is one exception to this rule in Company A). Work unit performance that depends on teamwork in Company C is believed by managers to be lower, but this has not been documented.

Unit Labor Cost—Either Higher or Lower

Unit labor cost for contingent workers—the combination of their compensation and their productivity—is a mixed bag. Sometimes it is lower, but the key finding is that sometimes it is higher for contingent workers. Lower wages do not necessarily make contingent workers cheaper. It depends on how much less their productivity is compared to their lower wages. Experience plays a role: Productivity is lower for contingent workers partly because they have less time on the job. Stability also plays a role: When teamwork is important, the churn of contingent workers coming and going gets in the way of good work unit performance.

The Extra Cost of Training

Training is usually needed for new contingent workers—at least some on-the-job training if not classroom training as well—and it might cost as little as a few hundred dollars or as much as a couple thousand dollars. This cost is not likely to be recovered by the company because the contingent workers usually do not stay on the job long enough. The cost of training is an extra cost of contingent labor. If other fixed employment costs like recruiting and selection are incurred, they also add to the expense.

The Cost-Effectiveness Question Mark

Contingent workers are surely not cost-effective if they have higher unit labor cost than core employees. They also are not cost-effective even if they have lower unit labor cost but their unrecovered training cost outweighs their unit labor cost saving. This is the finding in one of the companies, and it is probably true in a second company. This means that if the company is using contingent labor to save costs, then its expectations are not being realized. (Note that in one of the three companies, saving labor cost was one of two reasons to use contingent workers; in the other two cases, the reason was to match workforce to workload, not to save labor cost directly.) In the case of the company that uses contingent labor to quickly adjust the workforce to a fluctuating workload, the flexibility achieved comes with an expensive price tag attached.

Appendix to Case A: Calculating Training Costs, Cost Recovery, and Cost-Effectiveness for Contingent Workers

Training Costs

Training costs consist of direct cost plus opportunity cost, which is the wages paid to trainees less the value of output they produce during training.

- *Formal training from start date through three months*
  Direct cost to the company:
  Trainer's pay: $300–$360 per trainee
  > Formal training requires about 200 hours, usually delivered as five-hour training periods per day for three days per week over three months. This figure assumes that the trainer is paid $18,000 per year @ $9 per hour so that 200 training hours costs $1,800; assume that 5 to 6 trainees are trained at once so that each trainee incurs trainer costs of $300–$360.

  Equipment and space: assume no incremental cost
  Opportunity cost to the company:
  Wages paid to hourly part-time trainees = $1,250
  > Based on 200 hours over three months @ $6.25/hour

  Less value of output produced during training = $520
  > Based on 200 hours with 400 items per hour valued at $0.00648 per item.

  Output of 400 items per hour assumes output ranges from 0 to 800 items per hour during the training period; 800 items is the minimum requirement for successful completion of training. Value of $0.00648 per item is determined by equating 1,200 items per hour, which is the minimum rate of output to maintain employment as a trained proof operator, to $7.77, which is the wage rate to which a trained hourly part-time employee is raised who meets the 1,200 items per hour requirement.
  > Net opportunity cost = $730 ($1,250 − $520)
  > Formal training total cost to the company: $1,030 ($730 + $300) to $1,090 ($730 + $360) per trainee

- *On-the-job training from four months through nine months*
  Opportunity cost to the company
  Wages paid to hourly part-time employees = $3,250
  Based on $6.25/hour @ 20 hours/week for 26 weeks
  Less value of output produced = $3,370
  Based on 1,000 items per hour valued at $0.00648 per hour = $6.48 per hour, which is produced for six months = 26 weeks @ 20 hours per week. After formal training, employees must increase their output rate from 800 to 1,200 items per hour during the fourth through ninth months of service; the average output rate is 1,000 items per hour. The average workweek for hourly part-time employees is 20 hours.
  Net opportunity cost = − $120
- *Total training cost to the company*
  $910 ($1,030 − $120) to $970 ($1,090 − $120)

Recovery of Training Costs

Training costs begin to be recovered when the value of output produced by the trainee exceeds the wages paid to the trainee. The value of output and wages for full-time core employees and part-time contingent workers in one proof center in this company is shown in Figure 4-5.

- *Value of output produced after training is completed less wages paid:*

	Output rate per hour		
	1,200	1,300	1,400
Value of output produced ($ per hour)	$7.77	$8.42	$9.07
Wage paid ($ per hour)	7.77	7.77	8.10
Net payback rate ($ per hour)	0	.65	.97

Value of output produced is calculated at $0.00648 per item × output rate per hour. Incentive pay is paid for output rates in

Figure 4-5. Model of wage and output rates for core and contingent workers.

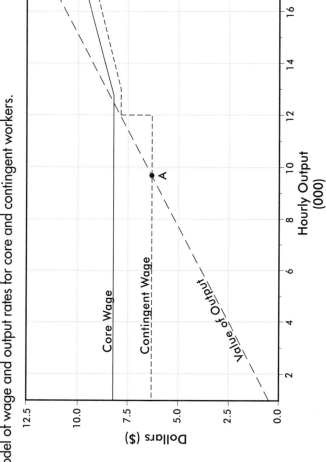

Notes: Value of output is $0.00648 per item, calculated by equating the experienced employee output requirement of 1,200 items per hour to the hourly part-time employee wage of $7.77 per hour. The wage rate for hourly employees rises from $6.25 to $7.77 per hour. At output rates exceeding 1,200 items per hour, the assumption is that the employee earns $0.35 per hour incentive pay for each additional 100 items per hour. Training cost recovery begins at point A when the value of output produced exceeds wages paid.

excess of 1,300 items per hour. The incentive pay is 33¢ per hour for each 100 items per hour beyond 1,300. This figure is based on the assumption that the company shares its "profits" from higher output rates equally with its employees, and 100 items per hour are worth 65¢.

• *Recovery of training costs by the company:*

	Output rate per hour		
	1,200	1,300	1,400
Payback period (hours)	infinite	1,445	970
Calendar time	infinite	2 yrs. 2 mo.	1 yr. 8 mo.
Training costs recovered	none	$270	$400

Calendar time is based on 20 hours per workweek for hourly part-time employees, to which is added the nine-month training period. Training costs recovered are determined by multiplying the net payback rate (see page 101) by the number of hours that trained workers put in before they quit, which is 410 hours (five months = 22 weeks @ 20 hours per week less holidays).

Cost-Effectiveness

Using the optimistic productivity figure of 1,400 items per hour, $400 of training cost is recovered, leaving $540 unrecovered. Since contingent workers stay on the job 410 hours after training is completed, spreading the unrecovered $540 over 410 hours yields an hourly figure of $1.32.

Appendix to Case B: The Cost of On-the-Job Training for Temporary Workers

One of the costs of on-the-job training is the output that is lost from supervisors while they are giving instruction to new workers. In the company's lockbox operations, a supervisor spends parts of three days this way:

Day	% of Output Lost	Value of Output Lost
1	75	$ 56.12
2	50	37.41
3	25	18.71
Total		$112.24

The value of output is determined to be $0.00778 per item, as follows: Assume that the value of output is equal to the wages and benefits of regular employees so that the company gets from employees just what it spends on them. Since wages and benefits are $10.12 an hour and output is 1,300 items an hour at the standard output rate, the value of output is $0.00778 per item. The value of output lost from supervisors is based on the actual average output rate of regular employees of 1,374 items an hour for seven hours a day valued at $0.0078 per item, which is $74.82 per day.

Another cost of on-the-job training is the cost of the wages and agency fee paid for temporary workers less the value of output they produce during training. This period lasts about four weeks during which trainees' output rate is assumed to increase linearly until it reaches the level achieved by experienced temporary workers (see Table 4-8 for a statistical interpretation of this information).

The total cost of on-the-job training is the sum of the lost output from the supervisor of $112.24 plus the wages less output from the trainee-worker of $149.76, which is $262 per trainee.

The payback period for recovering training costs is determined by dividing the total training cost of $262 by the cost recovery rate of $1.03 per hour. The cost recovery rate is the value of output produced by trained workers of $9.91, which is the average temporary worker output of 1,274 items per hour multiplied by $0.00778, less the temporary worker compensation cost of $8.88 per hour. $262 of training cost divided by $1.03 per hour yields 254 hours, which is ten calendar weeks (36 seven-hour days, or seven weeks and one day, scaled up by one-quarter to account for the fact that temporaries work three-quarters as much time as regular employees, and allowing also for holidays).

Table 4-8. Cost of lost output from trainees.

Day	Wage + Fee per Day	Output Produced as % of Experienced Temp Output	Value of Output	Net Cost of Training: Wage + Fee − Output
1	$62.16	25	$17.35	$44.81
2	62.16	25	17.35	44.81
3	62.16	50	34.69	27.47
4	62.16	75	52.04	10.12
5	62.16	75	52.04	10.12
6	62.16	77	53.43	8.73
7	62.16	78	54.12	8.04
8	62.16	80	55.50	6.66
9	62.16	82	56.89	5.27
10	62.16	83	57.59	4.57
11	62.16	85	58.97	3.19
12	62.16	87	60.36	1.80
13	62.16	88	61.04	1.12
14	62.16	90	62.44	−0.28
15	62.16	92	63.83	−1.67
16	62.16	93	64.52	−2.36
17	62.16	95	65.91	−3.75
18	62.16	97	67.30	−5.14
19	62.16	99	68.69	−6.53
20	62.16	100	69.38	−7.22
Total	$1,243.20		$1,093.38	$149.76

Note: The wage for new temporary workers is $7 an hour and the agency fee is $1.88 an hour, giving a total labor cost of $8.88 an hour or $62.16 a day. The value of output produced by trainees during training is based on the actual average output rate of experienced temporary workers of 1,274 items an hour for seven hours a day valued at $0.00778 per item, which is $69.38 per day.

Appendix to Case C: Calculating the Costs of Training for Contingent Workers

Initial Classroom Training

The total cost of initial classroom training for a contingent worker in an electronic assembly job is $478, composed of the following direct and opportunity costs:

- *Trainers' compensation:* $176 per contingent worker-trainee

  In 1991, 215 new contingent workers (representing 95 percent of the total contingent workforce of 225 people) received initial training. Since there are on average four trainees per class (the range is two to five), there were a total of 54 training classes during the year. The average training class is $3^2/_3$ days in duration (this is a weighted average for standard products assemblers, systems assemblers, and nonassembly workers, who each constitute roughly one-third of the workforce), which results in 198 training days, amounting to about 83 percent of the 240 working days in a year. A trainer's annual salary and benefits total about $45,600; 83 percent of that figure is $37,848. For 215 trainees, this yields a per trainee cost of about $176.

- *Consumable materials:* estimated to be about $10 per trainee
- *Facilities:* $74 per trainee

  The annual rental value of the training room and its equipment is estimated to be about $40,000. These facilities are used for initial classroom training and continuing training. The share of use devoted to initial training is about 40 percent, which amounts to $16,000. For 215 trainees, the cost is $74 per trainee per year.

- *Compensation paid to trainee:* $218 per contingent worker

  Contingent workers receive an average of $3^1/_3$ days of training, which amounts to $29^1/_3$ hours. Their cost to the company for wages and the agency fee is $7.44 per hour. For the initial training period, the total compensation cost is $218 per trainee.

(If core employees were hired directly from the external labor market as new employees, the foregone output cost of initial training for them would be: $3^2/_3$ days of training = $29^1/_3$ hours @ $8.89 per hour cost to company for wages and benefits = $261 per core employee-trainee. The total cost of initial classroom training for core employees would be $521.)

On-the-Job Training

The total cost of on-the-job training for contingent workers is $1,220, composed of the following opportunity costs:

- *Defective components and scrappage:* assumed to be zero
- *Value of foregone output from trainer:* $803

    A proportion of the certified trainer's usual output is lost because of time spent training a new worker. This proportion is shown in Table 4-9. The lost output is valued at the trainer's wage and benefit cost.

Table 4-9. Value of net foregone output during on-the-job training.

	Trainer		Trainee					
	Output Lost		Output Made		Wages Paid		Net Cost	
Week of Training	% (1)	Value (2)	% (3)	Value (4)	Contg. (5)	Core (6)	Contg. (5)−(4)	Core (6)−(4)
1st week	70	$312	20	$ 71	$ 298	$ 355	$227	$284
2nd week	50	223	40	142	298	355	156	213
3rd week	30	134	60	213	298	355	85	142
4th week	20	89	80	284	298	355	14	71
5th week	10	45	90	320	298	355	−22	35
6th week	0	0	100	355	298	355	−57	0
Total		$803		$1,385	$1,788	$2,130	$403	$745

Note: The proportion of output lost from the trainer and the proportion of output produced by trainees during on-the-job training is based on estimates from work unit managers coupled with learning curve expectations. The value of the trainer's lost output is based on the $18,000 median annual base salary of certified trainers plus benefits @ 28.5 percent to give a weekly compensation of $445. Wages paid to trainees are based on an actual entry-level hourly wage rate of $6 plus an agency fee of 24 percent to give weekly payment of $298. The value of output produced by trainees is based on the entry-level compensation paid to core employees of wages of $6.92 per hour plus benefits of 28.5 percent to give a weekly compensation of $355.

- *Net foregone output of contingent worker: $403*

    Wages and agency fees are paid during on-the-job training at the rate of $7.44 per hour, which totals $298 per week. For the six-week training period (we use the short end of the range of on-the-job training time), the total cost is $1,788.

    Contingent workers begin to produce output at increasing rates during the training period (see Table 4-9 for the output rates of contingent workers during on-the-job training). We value their output according to the compensation cost of core employees, which is $8.89 per hour or $355 per week. The total value of output produced by contingent workers during on-the-job training is $1,385. (If on-the-job training were provided to new core employees, the net foregone output cost would be $750. This figure is computed from their compensation cost during training of $2,130 less their value of output produced, $1,380. The total cost of on-the-job training for core employees would be $1,550.)

Continuing Classroom Training

The total cost of continuing classroom training for contingent workers is $415, consisting of the following direct and opportunity costs:

- *Trainers' compensation: $52 per trainee*

    The site has roughly 40 work teams, all of which take continuing training of about 5½ days duration, totaling 220 training days, which is 92 percent of the 240 working days in the year. A trainer's annual salary and benefits are about $45,600; 92 percent of that is $41,800. On average about 20 workers per work team or 800 workers in total receive continuing training, so the trainer's compensation cost per worker is about $52.
- *Consumable materials:* estimated to be $10 per trainee
- *Facilities:* $30 per trainee

    The annual rental value of the facilities is $40,000. The facilities are used for initial classroom training and continuing training. The share of use devoted to continuing training is about 60 percent, which amounts to $24,000. For 800 trainees, the cost is about $30 per trainee per year.

- *Compensation paid to contingent worker for continuing training:* $327

    Over a year an average of $5^1/_2$ days of continuing training is given to each worker, or 44 hours. The cost to the company for contingent labor is $7.44 per hour for wages and agency fee. The total compensation cost from continuing training is about $327 per worker per year.

[For core employees, compensation paid during continuing training is $390 (based on $8.89 per hour for wages and benefits). The total cost for continuing training for core employees is $483 per employee per year.]

Cost of Selecting Contingent Workers

The total selection cost per contingent worker is $80, consisting of opportunity costs as follows:

- *Manager's time:* $45 per new contingent worker
- *Team members' time:* $35 per new contingent worker

    The work unit manager interviews three candidates for one job @ $^1/_2$ hour each = $1^1/_2$ hours of time valued at $30 per hour, or $45 in total. Four or five team members interview two candidates for one job @ 20 minutes each = three hours valued at $11.50 per hour (average wage and benefits for experienced employees) = $35. This cost might be smaller if managers make up for the time they spend interviewing prospective contingent workers by putting in extra hours on their own projects, or if the time spent by team members interviewing prospective contingent workers increases their work team's productivity by fostering a sense of participation so that there is no lost output.

Recovery of Training Cost

If the average length of service of contingent workers is about seven months or 30 weeks, they work a total of 1,160 hours (allowing five days of holidays), which is 880 hours beyond the seven-week training period. The payback period is 46 weeks of service or 39 weeks after training is completed (see main chapter text). Therefore, the average contingent worker pays back $1.45 an hour for 880 hours = $1,275 of the total training cost of $2,183, leaving $908 in unrecovered cost. ($1.45 is the difference between wage cost and assumed value of output.) Of course, the unrecovered training cost is not lost to the company for those contingent workers who join the core workforce.

5

Managing for Cost-Effectiveness: Lessons From Experience

The cost-effectiveness of contingent labor is in doubt. The comfortable assumption of cheap temporary and part-time workers is not safe to make. It has to be checked out, case by case. Among the three companies whose experiences with contingent labor are reported in Chapter 4, one clearly is losing money on its contingent labor (Company A), one may very well be but cannot document it (Company C), and one is clearly saving money (Company B). While three cases, all with contingent workers in entry-level production jobs, do not permit a general conclusion to be drawn about cost-effectiveness, they do offer a compelling reason to search for ways to improve the cost picture for contingent labor.

What can managers do to improve the odds that contingent labor will be cost-effective? How can workforce flexibility be achieved at the lowest possible cost consistent with good performance? We suggest in this chapter a list of several actions that might be taken. Not all will apply to every work unit's situation, and some have better prospects for success than others.

The approach to finding managerial actions to improve cost-effectiveness is to look at the factors that determine it. We look at how to raise the productivity of contingent workers, reduce their training costs, and recover more of the training costs that are incurred. We begin by asking if it is possible to use fewer contingent workers in the first place.

Using Fewer Contingent Workers

Suppose the reason to have a contingent workforce is to match the size of the workforce to the size of the workload, or to create an employment security buffer around the core workforce. Then, if contingent labor is high-cost, the first way to cut costs is to try to use less of it. How can this be accomplished? Note that if cutting labor costs is itself the main reason to use contingent workers, but they turn out instead to be high-cost, then obviously the thing to do is to cut out the contingent workforce entirely.

Can You Smooth Out the Fluctuating Workload?

No company can change the business cycle and stop downturns from reducing its need for labor. But in some cases, unevenness in workload at any point in the business cycle can be smoothed out. If it can be, you remove the source of the problem and some of the need for contingent labor. The company in Case C did that by diversifying the industries of its customers. This is a matter of corporate strategy and marketing follow-through; it is probably out of the hands of a single work unit manager. For the banks in Cases A and B, workload smoothing was not a viable remedy. But in Company A, advanced operations management techniques were being explored to overcome the one-to-one linkage between fluctuating workload and human labor requirement.

Does the Contingent Workforce Track the Fluctuating Workload?

Look at your work unit's variation in output over time, and look at how many labor hours you get from contingent workers over time. Do they move together, as in the graph in Figure 3-2 (page 68)? Or do they move quite independently, as in the graph in Figure 5-1?

Figure 5-1, which illustrates the number of contingent workers against output, refers to one work unit in Company C. This unit has more temporary workers than it needs to match fluctuations in work-

Figure 5-1. Contingent workers and workload over time for one work unit in Company C.

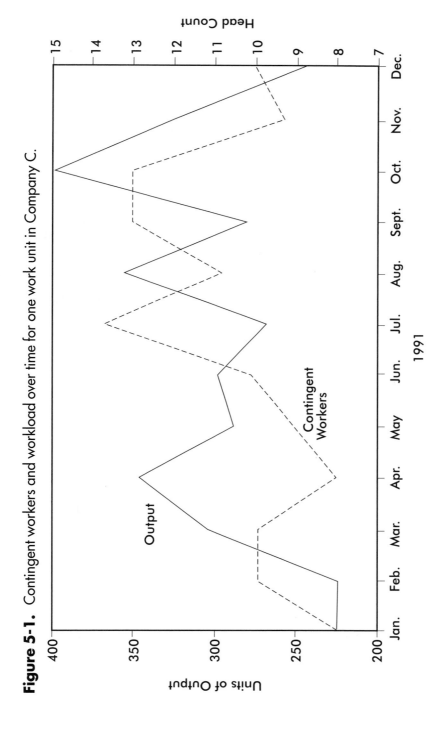

load and does not use temporaries primarily for this purpose anymore. In this work unit, the change in the number of contingent workers moves in the same direction as the change in output in only one period out of 12 (the correlation between the two variables is a low figure of only r = 0.14). If the contingent workforce does not change along with output, these workers are not actually giving you numerical flexibility after all. If so, you need to reduce the size of the contingent workforce.

Do You Have "Creeping Contingents"?

In some companies, the number of contingent workers just seems to grow and grow over time, apparently for no reason other than lack of attention and control. For example, managers in the company in Case C, which did smooth out its fluctuating workload, did not reduce the high proportion of their workforce accounted for by temporaries even though the need for them diminished. Observant managers call this phenomenon "creeping contingents." Two such managers expressed it to us this way:

> We got started several years ago with contingent labor when someone in the office of the chairman had the idea that we should have 5 percent contingent workers. So everyone raced around to find that many jobs, and they did, and the rest is history. Now we have 14 percent.

> In our business we think we're downsizing the core and we do that, and using a lot of external people creeps in. We don't want to hire regular full-time people because of our no-layoff policy, and then it looks like we're going to need more people—that's how you get creep.

Smart managers approach the question of the right size of their contingent workforce by asking: "How many contingent workers do we need to solve the business problem we have? What is the work that has to be done, and what is the best way to get it done?" (This is the reengineering approach, also discussed in the next section.) In most companies it is easier to get money (to pay for contingent workers) than it is to get time (an additional regular employee), and so the tendency is to overuse contingent workers. If contingent workers actually cost more, and they are not necessary to cope with fluctuating workloads, the easy way out is the wrong way out.

To solve the problem of creeping contingents requires two separate managerial decisions. The first decision is easy to declare but hard to implement: Downsize and reengineer the right way (see Chapter 2 for how downsizing relates to the contingent workforce). Don't downsize to the extent that you end up adding back more contingent workers than planned. The second decision is to abandon head count as a measuring stick, and use full-time equivalents instead. In particular, this change eliminates bias against using part-time employees in the core and thus overcomes one source of overuse of contingent workers.

Can You Reengineer the Work?

Reengineering is going on at most companies. If contingent labor is high-cost labor, evaluate the work that such employees do in your reengineering efforts. At the start, reengineering asks whether the work needs to be done at all. Then it asks how the work that is necessary should be done. The answer might be that some of the work should be outsourced—sometimes a form of contingent work. Or the answer might be to substitute machines for contingent labor, as one proof center manager in Company A is seeking to do. If the jobs that contingent workers do tend toward the routine, mechanistic, and repetitive, some of these tasks might be done instead by automated processes. Some of these jobs are bad jobs that might be eliminated by advanced technologies in the future. If so, the substitution of capital in the place of labor is good for the company and potentially good for core workers as well, although it forces contingent workers to find other jobs.

Can You Get Flexibility From the Core Workforce?

Contingent workers are not the only source of workforce flexibility. An additional margin of flexibility might be obtained from regular employees. Here we are thinking not just of the traditional use of overtime to add labor hours in peak demand periods. We are thinking also of other work scheduling and staffing alternatives. For example:

• *Work sharing instead of layoffs during the slack demand periods of business downturns.* Under work sharing plans, all workers cut back their hours (and pay) so that no workers will be laid off and lose out completely. This option, facilitated by labor law in only a few states in this country that allow partial (short-time) unemployment compensation, is widely used in Europe.

• *Work hours that can vary on short notice for core part-time employees within limits previously agreed on between worker and manager.* For example, let working time range from as little as 15 hours to as much as 30 hours a week. The company in Case A had this provision, although managers did not make extensive use of it.

• *Work-year contracts that allow a changing distribution over the year of a predetermined total number of hours.* This option gives the worker a certain annual income and the company some flexibility about when the work time is used. It is used occasionally in Europe, especially in Great Britain and Germany.

• *Voluntary reduced work time options for individual employees who cut back their work time and pay for a defined period of time, such as three months, subject to their supervisors' approval.* These programs, when adopted by companies, are called V-time. This option depends on the employee's initiative, but may also have some correspondence with the company's needs.

Each of these options has pluses and minuses. Each depends on employee preferences. Some are affected by labor law. Some are useful only for rather long swings in output, not day-to-day or week-to-week fluctuations. (See Chapter 2 for further discussion of the pros and cons of flexibility from the core workforce, and see AMACOM Book's *Creating a Flexible Workplace* by Olmsted and Smith, 1995, for extensive discussions of these options.) But keep in mind that just a small margin of new flexibility from the core workforce will ease the problem of high-cost contingent labor.

Raising the Productivity of Contingent Workers

One way to improve the cost-effectiveness of contingent workers is to raise their productivity and thereby lower their unit labor cost. The routes to higher individual productivity follow its fundamental determinants: ability or skill, and effort. How can these be improved?

Can You Get Contingent Workers With Better Skills?

One way to raise the skill level of the contingent workers you use is to do a better job of recruiting and selecting them, or to use temporaries from an agency that can meet your skill requirements. Whether this is possible to do depends on the characteristics of the people in the local labor market and the tightness of that labor market. If you do more recruiting and selecting, some additional administrative costs will be involved. And people with better skills are probably going to have more education, training, and experience, and that will undoubtedly mean higher wages, too.

Another way to raise the skill level of contingent workers is to do a better job of training them when they come to work for you, and then to provide incentives to keep them on the job longer. These are good ideas, although better training may cost too much more money, and lengthening the service time of contingent workers, if they are temporaries, is somewhat of a contradiction (more on this point in a later section in this chapter on "Recovering More Training Costs").

These approaches to raise the skill level of contingent workers have uncertain potential, not because better-skilled contingent workers cannot be located or created, but because the trade-off of higher skill with higher administrative and wage cost is uncertain.

An alternative solution to the problem of getting better contingent workers is to turn to temporary help services to supply contingent workers. A news story in *The Wall Street Journal* of June 24, 1994, reported on the experience of a growing small company in the machine tool industry that uses Manpower Temporary Services, the largest temporary help firm:

> Manpower recruits, tests, and hires assemblers and even skilled technicians. . . . "They kind of weed out the undesirables," said the assembly manager. . . . Corporations of all sizes have found that Manpower is far more efficient than they are at recruiting, training, and placing many entry-level workers.

All this service costs money—"Employers pay a 35 percent to 45 percent markup over the hourly wage to cover these and other Manpower expenses. . . . Throw in Manpower's administrative costs and room for a profit, and a $7 an hour job could cost the employer $10 an hour," according to the news story.

In the final analysis, whether you take steps to raise the productivity of contingent workers yourself or get the job done by a staffing company, the question remains the same: How much does it cost to raise productivity?

Can You Get More Effort From Contingent Workers?

People are likely to work harder if they are motivated, committed, and rewarded equitably. These are ways to get better work effort from contingent workers. However, commitment is going to be hard to get from contingent workers because in most cases it is not reciprocated by the company—there is no employment relationship, by definition. There is not a lot of involvement in the affairs of the workplace by contingent workers; they do not have an attachment to the employer. They do not expect to stay a long time; they have no employment security. To get a psychological type of commitment from a contingent worker to the company looks like an uphill struggle.

(An exception to the general presumption about low commitment is the case of contingent workers who are specialized high-level professionals. Their commitment is to their profession, and they are likely to put forth a good effort stemming from professional pride. If their work is fairly autonomous, commitment to the company is not so important.)

Can You Link Pay to Performance?

Another type of commitment—economic or transactions commitment—might be obtained and used to induce hard work. The way in which workers are rewarded affects their effort, and wages are a principal reward. Instead of paying people a straight wage only, can you offer them performance-related pay or incentive pay? The incentive might be individual, based on output rate, as is done as a matter of policy in the company in Case A (an extra 100 items of output an hour earns an extra 33¢ an hour), or as is done as a matter of the supervisor's discretion in the company in Case B (where productivity-based wage raises go as high as $1 an hour or 15 percent above standard wage rates). The incentive might be a group incentive if teamwork is important to work unit performance.

Can You Offer Regular Employment to the Best Contingent Workers?

A second type of reward can affect effort: If the contingent worker hopes to obtain regular employment in the company in the near future, then surely he or she will try hard to be a good worker. Therefore, a practice of hiring regular employees from the contingent workforce may raise the productivity of the contingent workforce. This is a feasible practice because a sizable number of contingent workers (about one-third of all temporary workers) take up jobs with this status precisely because they see it as a way into regular employment.

Hiring from the contingent ring into the regular core is illustrated by Avon Products, a major U.S. consumer products company that maintains a sizable "reserve" workforce alongside its regular workforce for manufacturing and distribution operations in the United States. The reserve workforce, composed mostly of women who work on an on-call basis, exists mainly to adjust labor input to seasonally changing workloads. But all of the new entrants into the regular workforce come from the reserve workforce, after a wait of up to three years. Avon claims that its two workforces are the same in terms of productivity.

However, the ring-into-core concept can also be opposed. For example, Hewlett-Packard's early guidelines for its contingent workforce did not allow contingent workers to become regular employees until six months passed since they stopped being HP contingent workers. The rationale was a desire that the contingent workforce be composed of people who voluntarily chose this status. It was not supposed to be a screening pool for new hires into the regular workforce. However, HP managers wanted to be able to hire the best of the contingent workers they saw. In the end, a new structure for contingent labor was developed without the ban on movement from ring to core.

Should You Give Equal Pay for Equal Work?

This is a tough question that has two controversial sides. On the one hand, if core and contingent workers really do the same job but the contingent workers get smaller wages and benefits, some of them will begin to feel mistreated and may slack off. As one manager told us:

Outside employees start to feel an expectation. They think to themselves, why shouldn't I get paid for the day off? I come here and work and do the same things they [regular employees] do. They begin to expect that they are an employee if they've been around a long enough time.

A graphic account of low-paid temporaries who stopped working up to their potential was related in *Fortune* magazine of January 24, 1994, p. 36:

Desperate to curb labor costs, Kolmar Laboratories, a cosmetics maker in Port Jervis, New York, began filling openings and covering work surges with temps. By the summer of 1992, roughly half of its 600 assembly line workers were temps. . . . These temps, who earned $5.60 an hour with no benefits, worked in teams with permanent employees who received, for the same work, up to $9 an hour plus benefits, depending on their output. Fights broke out regularly between the two groups. . . . All day long people shouted, "Go faster; you're holding us up." But the temps had no incentive to work faster.

The other side of the controversy about equal treatment of contingent versus core people is that some core employees feel they should have some status or privileges not available to contingent workers. These core employees believe that their long service to the company entitles them to a few advantages. They believe, at the very least, that they should have first choice at the best jobs. If some status differences are not maintained, discontent can arise among core employees. The resentment can also be reversed when core employees feel that contingent workers are in a more favorable position because of better pay or access to job openings.

The way out of this controversy begins by recognizing that the key word is equity, not equality. If the objective is to extract quality work from contingent workers, they must feel equitably treated. That does not necessarily mean equal wages and benefits. For example, Company A pays its contingent part-time employees a 10 percent wage premium as a partial substitute for benefits. They do not receive equal compensation. But many of these contingent workers are young. They do not care about retirement plans that provide income far into the future; they need income now. For these people, an extra 70¢ an hour is probably a good subjective trade-off against benefits. [Caution: The net value of a missing retirement package (not calculated here) accumulated over a working lifetime is probably more than 70¢ an hour even in present value terms so that rationally the trade-off of substituting pay today for benefits tomorrow is probably a bad one.]

Reducing Training Costs

Because the cost of training new contingent workers is substantial in many cases, it is important to look for ways to minimize this cost. Three alternatives, which are described in the sections that follow, come to mind.

Can You Hire Already-Trained Workers?

Two approaches are possible; they are the same as first described in the section entitled "Can You Get Contingent Workers With Better Skills?" If the contingent workers are part-time employees, try to recruit and select people who are already trained in the type of work that needs to be done. This will add some administrative costs, and will depend for its success on the local labor market. Or, if the contingent workers are temporaries from an agency, can you shift the training task to the agency? The company in Case B was able to keep its training costs down to a low $260 per new contingent worker because its temporary help agency was able to supply people with prior data entry experience or to train them in this type of work beforehand.

Can You Do Less Training?

If new contingent workers come to you already trained, of course you can minimize the amount of training you do. If they do not come fully trained, can you still reduce training? Yes, if you can simplify the work to be done by using advanced technologies, with automated processes taking over some of the routine tasks otherwise done by people. This is an attractive prospect for the bank in Case A, which was investigating optical scanning techniques to eliminate some of the human manual labor in data entry work. Cautions need to be issued here, however. Too much "scientific management" and too much job simplification—Taylorism run amok—reduce productivity. There is a limit to how simple jobs should be made. Additionally, installing new technologies is potentially costly itself.

Can You Reduce the Lost Output Portion of Training Cost?

The largest part of the total training cost is usually the lost output from supervisors during on-the-job training and from the trainees themselves when they are not producing much or any output but still being paid a wage. This suggests that a lower training wage be paid to new contingent workers during their training period and that they receive a higher wage after training is successfully completed. In fact, the bank in Case A reduces its training costs by hundreds of dollars per worker in this way. A way to reduce lost output costs from supervisors is to try to conduct on-the-job training for more than one new contingent worker at a time.

Recovering More Training Costs

Training costs are recovered if two conditions are met: (1) If the value of output produced by trained workers exceeds the compensation they are paid, and (2) if the trained workers stay on the job or with the company long enough. The value of output produced depends on productivity, which we have already discussed in this chapter. What about the second source of training cost recovery? Can we get trained contingent workers to stay on the job long enough to pay back their training cost?

Here we face a fundamental contradiction: Contingent workers are not intended to be long-service workers. That is neither their intent nor the company's (setting aside for the moment the problem of the abuse of "permanent" temporaries). Companies do not expect to give 25-year service pins and gold watches to contingent workers. And contingent workers have other life interests outside their current job that will change, such as school, child care, a spouse's situation; they will of their own volition leave the job sooner rather than later. However, some actions can be taken to reduce premature resignations and increase the likelihood that contingent workers will stay on the job long enough to pay back more if not all of their training costs. We suggest four options in the sections to follow.

Can You Design Benefits Tailored to Contingent Workers' Needs?

Paying no benefits to contingent workers is cheaper and simpler in the very short run than working out some sort of prorated benefits package. But maybe paying some benefits with features attractive to some contingent workers is smart in the longer run. Look at this example, reported in the Labor Letter column of *The Wall Street Journal* of November 12, 1991, page 1:

> Paying college expenses for workers helps Carl's Jr., a 600-restaurant chain, keep employees longer. In a two-year test at 43 California restaurants, the chain saved $145,128 in turnover costs, while spending $90,000 on workers' tuition and other education fees.

Although the experience of Carl's Jr. refers to all employees, not specifically to contingent workers, it illustrates the point. If your contingent workers are part-timers and many of them are college students, as is true for the bank in Case A, the tuition benefit may keep them employed until they finish college (which could be a low-tuition community college or state-subsidized university), and that may be long enough to pay back their training costs.

Can You Convert Some Contingent Workers to Core Employees?

Offering contingent workers access to regular employment in the core was discussed previously as one way to increase their productivity by increasing their effort. The same practice has a second advantage. If converting a contingent worker to core employee prevents a premature resignation, then the training investment is not lost; the chance to recover the training cost is saved. Even if that converted person also changes jobs or work units within the same company and therefore does not use all of the training provided earlier, the company saves some of the cost of training a totally new core employee. This argues in favor of permeability between core and ring so that new contingent workers who really want regular employment have a realistic chance of obtaining it before they quit. In essence, the worker's job in the contingent workforce is the first step in a potential career with the company. Both Companies B and C hire trained contingent workers into their regular workforce; in fact it is the only way in for the data entry and assembly jobs in the work units we studied. No initial training is given to core employees because there are no new core employees.

Can You Offer Short-Term Contracts?

One way to reduce uncertainty on both the workers' part and the company's part about length of service is to give contingent workers contracts of a specified duration. The contracts might be three months or six months long and renewable, or they might specify a minimum and maximum number of hours to be worked. This method of employing contingent labor is commonplace in Europe. Although such a contractual approach might abridge somewhat the company's flexibility to add and subtract labor (staggered contract end dates among the contingent workers can help out), there is a compensating benefit—both longer and more predictable time on the job by contingent workers.

Can You Link Pay to Time on the Job?

Contingent workers rarely get a wage increase based on length of service, although such increases (for example, cost-of-living increases) are quite common for core employees. No doubt this is true because contingent workers are unlikely to stay with the company longer than one year, which is the usual length of time for service-based pay increases. Nevertheless, a modest incentive to stay on the job long enough to pay back training costs, delivered in the form of a wage increase after a specified number of hours or months worked, is an approach to consider.

Company C had an informal expectation that its temporary workers should stay on the job for nine months (or up to one year); that length of time on the job would permit all of the high training costs to be recovered. But because there was no tangible reward from the company, few did so.

Summing Up: A Checklist for Managers

If contingent labor is high-cost as currently used, several approaches can be considered to improve the cost-effectiveness of your work unit. Here is a brief list of some potential actions:

- Reduce the need for contingent workers by smoothing out the fluctuations in the workload.
- Check if the number of contingent workers has become larger than necessary to meet your flexibility needs.
- Prevent excessive downsizing that would generate unintended demand for contingent workers.
- Use full-time equivalents instead of head count to measure employment so that bias against core part-time employment is reduced.
- Substitute capital for labor when outmoded jobs done by contingent workers can be eliminated by advanced technologies.
- Get a margin of flexibility from regular employees via work sharing, variable hours for core part-timers, work-year contracts, and voluntary reduced work time options.
- Improve recruiting, selection, and training of contingent workers if you can do so without raising administrative or wage costs too much.
- Use temporary help firms to provide better-skilled contingent workers if they can do the human resources management tasks better or cheaper than you can.
- Link some contingent workers' pay to their performance as an incentive to do good work.
- Offer regular employment to the best contingent workers as an incentive to do good work and as a way to prevent premature resignations and save training costs.
- Pay equitable if not equal wages and benefits to some contingent workers to improve their motivation; offer benefits to contingent workers that appeal especially to their needs.
- Hire already-trained workers into your contingent workforce to minimize the training costs you incur, unless the wage is too high.
- Simplify the jobs that contingent workers do, up to a point, to minimize the training required.

- Pay a lower wage during training and a higher wage after training to reduce training costs.
- Hire contingent workers on a short-term contractual basis to reduce uncertainty about time on the job.
- Reward contingent workers who stay on the job long enough to pay back their training costs with pay tied partly to length of service.

6

Managing With the Workers in Mind

To increase workforce flexibility and to do it cost-effectively means answering questions about company strategy. In Chapter 2, we looked at contingent work from a company perspective, examining business objectives and strategies for fitting part-time, temporary, and contract labor into the workforce. We suggested questions to ask about the way you currently use contingent workers and how these arrangements might be improved—questions about what type of work is to be done, what type of staffing (part-time, temporary, short-term contract) fits your needs, how many contingent workers to use, whether contingent and core workers do the same jobs, what local labor market conditions are like, and others.

In this chapter we focus on the contingent workers themselves. How can they be managed so that they do the best possible job for you cost-effectively? Like regular employees, contingent workers need to be managed—not as much, perhaps, as regular employees because for some companies less management is part of the reason to have them in the first place. But less management is not no management. We know, for example, that if contingent workers turn in subpar performance, lack of supervision may be one of the factors that explains it.[1]

Issues for Managers

Among various issues in managing contingent workers, we look at a few that company experiences show are most likely to materialize.

147

How much pay and benefits and privileges should contingent work-ers get? Should they be appraised and rewarded for merit, length of service, or both? How should contingent workers relate to core employees? How separate are they? Should contingent workers be a recruiting pool for core employees? These are issues that affect busi-ness performance and cost.

It is not only issues of business performance and cost that con-front managers. There are larger issues outside the company—issues about the equity with which contingent workers are treated, and about the long-term impact of contingent labor on labor markets and on the social fabric of the country. Well-known business leader Sid-ney Harman, Chairman of Harman Industries, was quoted by Robert Kuttner in *Business Week,* October 18, 1993, as saying:

> Temps are bad for the economy; they're unfair and set up a second class of employee.

Granted, Sidney Harman is not a typical CEO, and Robert Kutt-ner can safely be tagged left of center. But consider what the business section of the *Economist*—the forthrightly libertarian British news magazine—said in an April 3, 1993, article entitled "The Death of Corporate Loyalty":

> Although superficial damage will eventually fade, the insti-tutional costs of forsaking the old links between employees and their companies could take even longer to emerge.

The growing use of contingent labor, the continuing trend toward downsizing and reengineering, and the possible end of the old psychological contract between company and employee inevita-bly combine to draw the attention of public policy makers. Legisla-tion is periodically introduced in the U.S. Congress to regulate the conditions of employment of part-time workers (although it has not come close to passing), and the Internal Revenue Service steps up its enforcement of the misuse of independent contractors by companies. Forward-thinking managers will want to use contingent labor wisely so that the interests of public policy and business are not at odds.

This chapter suggests ways to manage contingent workers both cost-effectively and equitably, with an eye toward how the use of contingent labor affects institutions and society, and therefore also businesses themselves, in the long run.

A case study of an experience at Hewlett-Packard and one at Avon Products examine the practices of leading companies. They illustrate important issues that arise when thoughtful managers implement major contingent worker programs. Both cases deal with contingent workers in a range of factory and office jobs, but not as technically specialized independent contractors.

—————————————— **CASE STUDY** ——————————————

THE CASE OF HEWLETT-PACKARD[2]

Hewlett-Packard is an acknowledged leader in the development and quality of its products as well as in the management of its workforce. It tries to give its people employment security, and has never yet had a mass layoff since its founding in 1939. It was one of the first companies in the United States with a flextime program. Like other companies, Hewlett-Packard uses contingent labor.

The computer industry downturn of 1985 and 1986 showed Hewlett-Packard how much it needed workforce flexibility. HP needed to be able to vary labor input up and down around a base core employment level—a core-ring idea—as demand for its products varied cyclically and unpredictably.

But there was more to it than that. HP's businesses shift very rapidly because of turbulent markets and rapidly changing technology. When a new product is launched, HP may not be able to add regular employees fast enough or may not want to do so until the product is sure to succeed. Contingent workers could be used during the ramp-up. Also, when other businesses are being phased out, contingent workers are needed to replace the regular employees who are gradually being moved out. Even if staffing levels overall are stable, work units come and go, and people need to be quickly added and subtracted within a plant or division. Flexible staffing is a priority.

To achieve flexibility, HP follows a sequence of actions. For example, if a reduction in workforce is needed at a plant:

1. Overtime is reduced to zero (it often runs at a high 7 percent of base hours at some HP plants).
2. Temporaries from staffing companies are sent back.

3. Contingent workers who are employees are reduced in number.
4. Core employees are offered relocation, voluntary severance, or early retirement.
5. Work from another plant is shifted to the plant with slack work.
6. Work sharing for core full-time and part-time employees is adopted.
7. Work done by subcontractors or vendors is taken in-house to the extent possible (e.g., food service, custodial service, some component supplies).

The contingent worker program that was developed by HP to give the company more flexibility—the second and third actions in the preceding sequence—was called "FlexForce."

FlexForce—How It Worked

The FlexForce contingent labor program started in the fall of 1988. It was created by a task force that included manufacturing managers and general managers as well as human resources managers. Flex-Force consisted of hourly part-time employees and in-house or direct-hire temporaries:

- "On-call" people were part-timers on the HP payroll who worked up to 1,400 hours a year on full-day but part-month or part-year schedules; their work schedules could be changed by their managers at will; they could work on-call indefinitely.
- "On-contract" people were direct-hire temporaries on the HP payroll who worked full-time schedules for contract periods up to six months renewable to a maximum length of service of two years.

FlexForce also incorporated temporaries from staffing companies and independent contractors who had previously been used, but guidelines about when and how they were to be used were clarified.

Companywide in the United States, on-call and on-contract employees for Hewlett-Packard grew to about 2,700 people or 3 percent of HP's total workforce in 1991, about evenly split between the two categories. They worked in all sorts of business units from manufacturing to sales, and did all sorts of jobs from telemarketing to engineering. Agency temporaries and independent contractors not on the payroll added another 2,300 people. Corporate guidelines said that contingent workforce numbers shouldn't go beyond 10 percent of HP's total U.S. workforce (it actually reached 5 to 6 percent), or beyond 15 percent at any one site.

Pay for on-call and on-contract FlexForce employees consisted of wages at the midpoint, not the entry level, of the job grade to which they were assigned. This amounted to premium pay of about 15 percent above entry level for those FlexForce employees whose skill and experience would otherwise have put them at the entry level for the job they were hired to do. Although HP tried to hire people who were ready to work, it was often the case that some additional training was necessary.

Pay increases for on-call and on-contract employees were sometimes awarded on the basis of a simple "check the box" appraisal—satisfactory or unsatisfactory on quality, productivity, dependability and attendance, teamwork, flexibility, and overall performance. This simple appraisal and pay system was kept separate from the core employee compensation system.

No benefits were paid to any FlexForce employees, except of course those mandated by law (social security, workers' compensation, and unemployment insurance). Since benefits for core employees amounted to about 40 percent of base wages for core employees, the total compensation for FlexForce people was clearly less despite the wage premium that applied to most of them. Some privileges of employment available to core employees, such as membership in the company credit union, were extended to FlexForce employees, but others were not, such as subsidized transit passes.

A rather large proportion of on-call and on-contract employees were college students; they were able to quickly pick up the technical skills often required and could work irregular schedules as well as weekday daytime hours. In fact, HP came to believe that the success of FlexForce depended partly on an ample supply of students in the labor market where a site was located. Many FlexForce people were also second income earners in a family or retired people, especially military retirees.

FlexForce—Why It Didn't Last

The Hewlett-Packard FlexForce ended in 1994 after a run of six years. It was replaced by a new scheme that relies wholly on temporaries from staffing companies. FlexForce ended even though it succeeded in achieving the amount and type of flexibility that the company needed. It ended even though company management noted that the business units that used more FlexForce employees had higher profitability than those that used fewer FlexForce employees. (Managers also noted that this might have been a chicken-and-egg result and didn't credit FlexForce with the profit outcomes.) Despite the pros of FlexForce, several major issues arose in the management of FlexForce contingent workers that proved problematic.

Labor Supply—Ample But Wrong

The number of people available for contingent labor jobs was ample, but they weren't the right kind of people. Hewlett-Packard's idea in the creation of a ring of contingent workers around the core was that the two would be separate. Mobility between core and contingent workforces was strongly discouraged. FlexForce employees could not convert to core employment until after one year in the FlexForce. Core employees, whether full-time or part-time, could go into the FlexForce, but not back into the core. The intention was that each workforce should be occupied by people who preferred that status; FlexForce people should prefer good temporary or casual part-time work that did not carry the implied obligations of core employment. The limited movement from ring to core would ensure that the ring contained the right people. To join the FlexForce they had to choose to be contingent as a way of working rather than as an entree into core employment.

But the number of people who preferred contingent work wasn't there. There weren't enough second income earners who were covered by a spouse's benefits or students with no interest in benefits. About half the FlexForce people really wanted to be core employees, according to the impressions of HP managers. FlexForce applicants were interviewed, and managers sought to determine their employment motivations and expectations. But even if an applicant genuinely wanted an arm's-length relationship with the company before coming to work, that very same person might change after being at work for a few months.

Consequently, pockets of sizable groups of FlexForce employees built up in some locations or work units and these employees began to ask HP to help them as a group to buy benefits that HP didn't provide to them, such as group health and life insurance. The company declined to help in this way, but also was unwilling to incur discontent among FlexForce employees. It seemed that an alternative to FlexForce was advisable.

Managers' Preferences—Contingent Labor as a Screening Device

The company did not intend to use FlexForce as a way to screen potential recruits into the core. "Don't allow FlexForce to become a screening device or a trial period for regular employees," was the advice from corporate human resources people. But managers found the bar to mobility from ring to core to be an unnatural constraint on their ability to choose the best people they could for regular jobs. Perhaps reliance on a pool of contingent workers for sourcing core employees is unwise in the long run—managers should not lose touch with the external labor market and default on their recruiting and selecting responsibilities. But day to day, managers who saw good contingent employees wanted to bring them into the core; often the contingent employee wanted that as well. The distinction between core and ring began to break down.

Culture Clash—Separate and Unequal

For a long time, Hewlett-Packard has cultivated a "people philosophy"—a corporate culture that stresses informality, sharing, participation, and teamwork. The centerpiece is a formally stated corporate objective ". . . to provide employment security (for our people) based on their performance" (from the Hewlett-Packard *1989 Annual Report*). The company's people philosophy is captured in the "HP Way" that is expressed in company publications:

> What Is the HP Way? . . . Bill Hewlett once put it this way: "I feel that in general terms it is policies and actions that flow from the belief that men and women want to do a good job and that if they are provided the proper environ-

ment they will do so. Closely coupled with this is the tradition of treating each individual with consideration and respect, and recognizing individual achievements." [The company has] an inner core of shared values: trust, . . . teamwork in achieving common objectives (from *The Test of Time*, March 1989).

HP's openness and informality contribute to a non-authoritarian atmosphere (from *HP in Brief*, February 1991).

FlexForce challenged the "HP Way." Were FlexForce people company people? Officially, yes, because they were employees on the payroll. On the factory floor or in the office, they were indistinguishable from regular employees. But in fact they were not the same as regular employees. They could not be attached to the company in the "HP Way." Their separateness was enforced. They could get neither the commuting subsidy nor business cards. They could not participate in certain staff meetings or some company social events. Because on-contract employees had contracts that lasted six months maximum and might not be renewed, they could hardly be fully participating team members.

Inside the work units, some managers wondered if a potentially divisive two-tier workforce was being created—core employees with benefits and security, and contingent workers with neither, but who wanted both. More than most companies, Hewlett-Packard, which was nonunion at most of its manufacturing locations, did not like the outlook. Separate and unequal was a tough message to deliver.

Some managers also found it increasingly hard to let FlexForce employees go when the need for them ended, especially if they had made efforts to include them as team members. Since these employees worked only at HP while they were in the FlexForce, they had no other job to go to immediately. Some managers felt a responsibility for their employment future.

Preferred Providers—The New Contingent Workforce Plan

In 1994, the Hewlett-Packard approach to contingent labor changed. Contingent workers continue to be used in substantial numbers (they amount to about 7 percent of the HP workforce in the United States), and for the same purposes. But they are managed differently. Contingent workers are no longer employees on the HP payroll. Instead they are supplied as temporaries from staffing companies. While there is nothing new about that sort of arrangement, there is a new relationship between HP and the staffing companies.

Staffing Companies as Partners

The new HP approach to contingent labor embodies a view of staffing companies as partners in obtaining and managing contingent workers. Staffing companies are not seen as old-style agencies that send over fill-ins on short notice when someone else is out sick or on vacation (although that still happens). Instead HP establishes long-term relationships with a small number of preferred providers. In return for substantial business with HP, the staffing company agrees to meet certain HP expectations about how it handles the contingent workers. This means, at the very least, that the staffing company pays a benefits package and provides training. The workers HP gets are expected to be above average. The two-year maximum length of service rule remains.

An essential part of the relationship between HP and the staffing company is that the staffing company puts its representative on-site full-time at the HP factory or office that uses sizable numbers of the staffing company's people. HP provides the space; the staffing company pays the salary. Three purposes are served by the staffing company's on-site coordinator:

1. The on-site coordinator is a partial supervisor for the contingent workers, lifting some of these tasks from HP managers; the on-site coordinator assists in directing the contingent workers and is a person to whom they can go with problems about their work situation.
2. The on-site coordinator enables HP managers to do a better job of getting the right contingent workers because he or she has ongoing face-to-face contact with HP managers and workplace needs.
3. Potential legal issues of co-employment are minimized. (Legal issues are discussed further in Chapter 7.)

How Costs Are Viewed

The HP plan with staffing companies is not on the surface the cheapest way to manage contingent workers. Benefits, training, and on-site supervision, even if provided by a staffing company, are not free to HP. But cost is not the driver. HP's objective in utilizing contingent labor is to achieve flexibility—to buffer the core workforce and cope with rapid change in the need for labor. Paying smaller wages and benefits or cutting fees to staffing companies is not the objective.

In fact, HP does not want to give managers a wage incentive to misuse or overuse contingent workers. Contingent labor is not intended to be cheaper than core employment. Contingent workers cost managers as much in payments to suppliers as regular employees cost in wages and benefits. Therefore, the incentive to use contingent workers is not to reduce cost. It is to use them properly in order to attain the flexibility that provides employment security for core employees. The payoff from contingent labor is the flexibility it gives, not the cost it saves.[3] HP wants the best contingent workers available, and HP wants these contingent workers to be treated equitably. Whether that costs more or less is not decisive.[4]

Relief From the Culture Clash

The advent of preferred providers who supply most of Hewlett-Packard's needs for contingent labor takes care of some of the previous uneasiness about the enforced separation of the contingent workforce from core employment. Now, contingent workers from staffing companies really are separate—they are not HP employees; they belong to the staffing company, although HP is the job-site employer.

That does not mean they cannot become HP employees. HP has established a method for determining when and how contingent workers can do so. In the example of a successful new product ramp-up to a predicted stable output and employment level, some of the work done by contingent workers will be converted to regular employment with jobs filled in the following order: first, redeployed employees from other HP locations; second, internal job postings for 10 days; and third, external recruiting, including contingent workers currently at HP from a staffing company. The contingent workers might have an advantage over the actual external recruits because of their experience and record with HP.

The fact that contingent workers are not HP employees and that they are presumably equitably treated by their staffing company eases some of the culture clash previously felt by some HP managers. If the contingent workers really get adequate pay and benefits and training from their staffing company, have their own "supervisor" on-site, and have other employment options when they leave their assignments at HP, then they are separate but not so unequal. It all depends on the terms of the relationship between HP and the staffing company.

The shift to staffing companies does not take away all of the culture clash. Contingent workers still will have a hard time functioning as team members, and an impression of a two-tier workforce might still remain.

Lessons Learned

The experiences of Hewlett-Packard in managing contingent workers raise some questions and provide some answers. While the case of one company cannot be applied across the board to other companies, the lessons learned from a recognized industry leader merit other managers' attention.

For HP, the purpose served by contingent labor is flexibility, and the reason why flexibility is needed is mainly to buffer the core workforce. HP does not want contingent labor to be cheaper than core employment, when cost is viewed narrowly as wages and benefits. That would distract managers' decisions from the true purpose for contingent labor.

It takes a special type of person to prefer contingent worker status to core employee status, and in HP's experience, there are not enough of these people in the labor market. Therefore the problem (or is it the opportunity?) of taking contingent workers into regular employment has to be faced. Even if premium pay is awarded as a partial substitute for benefits, the desired balance between supply and demand does not take shape.

Company culture, if it really embodies positive human relations notions such as participation, teamwork, sharing, and inclusiveness, does not match up very well with the use of contingent labor. Managers and supervisors who work day in and day out with contingent workers find it difficult to treat them differently. Formal policies and procedures are one thing; informal practices are quite another. Cul-

ture is powerful. In the end, culture clash caused HP to change the
way it managed its contingent workforce.

For HP, the way to manage contingent labor equitably is to work
through a small number of staffing companies as preferred providers
who measure up to HP's expectations. The task of providing good
human resources management services—including pay, benefits,
training, and some on-site supervision—is carried out by the staffing
companies according to HP specifications. This makes contingent
workers as separate from the core workforce as possible, but it also
makes them more equal.

———— CASE STUDY ————

THE CASE OF AVON PRODUCTS[5]

Avon is a household word. The company is a major force in the consumer products business worldwide. But some markets (for example,
the United States, Canada, and Europe) are mature, and margins are
thin. Growth is hard to achieve, and costs are critical. There are significant growth opportunities in several global markets. The business
is seasonal, with peak demand in the holiday-rich fourth quarter. The
company's need for contingent labor fluctuates widely over the year.
Workforce flexibility is needed to match labor supply to the fairly
predictable peaks and valleys in labor demand. It must be achieved
cost-effectively because labor is a sizable share of total cost. And it
must be achieved through good practices because Avon has to be a
good employer with a good name in the fickle retail market.

A distribution facility on the East Coast illustrates the problem.
Thousands of orders come in from the field every day. They must
be assembled, packaged, and shipped within two days. Because the
business is seasonal, fourth quarter shipments might be twice as great
as first quarter shipments. Products are manufactured at other company locations in the United States, and some items are imported
from other companies in other countries. Very little inventory of
products is kept because there are too many of them (more than 800)
that are produced in huge volumes (millions of pieces per year).
Every order is a unique combination of products that is assembled
when it is received; there is no prepackaging. Therefore the linkage
between orders and labor hours is direct and tight.

Avon needs to add and subtract labor hours over the year, and managers do so through the use of a contingent workforce. Avon does not want to use overtime at premium pay to get more hours from regular employees, and Avon does not want to lay off regular employees during slack times of the year and then try to recall them. Avon does not use work sharing cyclically either. Temporaries from staffing companies are used to supplement core staff in some locations.

Reserves—Contingent Part-Timers

Avon's contingent workers, called "reserves," are on-call employees who are on the company payroll. They usually work full days when they are called in, but most of them do not work year around. (The reserves could be termed direct-hire temporaries except that they tend to stick with one job in the plant instead of rotate, and they are fairly long-serving employees.) Reserves are on-call because whether or not they work on any given day depends on their manager's need for them.

In the East Coast facility, peak workloads are customarily met by adding reserves to the main day shift (7:00 A.M. to 3:45 P.M.) and expanding the smaller second shift (4 P.M. to 12:30 A.M.). In this facility, the average employment level over the year is about 900, and reserves account for more than a quarter of all labor hours hired during the fourth quarter.

Because the workload fluctuates seasonally and is fairly predictable, many reserves are likely to work full-time hours without interruption for several months. Who is called in depends on seniority, so reserves with a year or so of service can predict when and how much they will work. The average reserve employee works from 1,300 to 1,900 hours a year at the East Coast plant, depending on the amount of business in that particular year.

The jobs that reserves do are often the same jobs that regular employees do, in both the office and the plant. Nevertheless, there are no reserves in the highest-graded jobs.

Almost all the reserves are women in this plant, but this fact is unremarkable because facilitywide, 86 percent of all employees are women. It is also noteworthy that 65 percent of all the managers at this facility are women.

How Contingent Workers Are Managed

Two aspects of the management of the contingent reserves merit special attention: their wages and benefits, and their relationship to the regular workforce. Differences between core and contingent workers, as you will see, are very small. Managing one is very much like managing the other.

Wages and Benefits

The rule for Avon contingent workers is equal pay for equal work, and nearly equal benefits. Reserves get exactly the same rate of pay as regular employees when they do the same job, and they can get wage increases on the same basis as regular employees. In the East Coast plant, wage raises are first granted after one year of service. The average length of service of reserves here is nearly $3^1/2$ years, so many do get wage increases (regular employees have 13 years of service on the average).

However, since few reserves work full-time year-round, it typically takes longer than one calendar year—probably 13 to 20 months—for them to be eligible for their first wage increase. And because of their shorter length of service, some reserves actually get less pay even when in the same job as a regular employee, but this difference is due solely to less length of service, not pay practices. This is an expected outcome for regular part-time employees as well as contingent part-timers.

Contingent workers at the East Coast facility earn benefits according to hours worked. The first benefits are paid after 500 hours are worked in a year, and additional benefits are paid after 1,000 hours. These benefits include health insurance (for which reserves contribute an extra $120 a year because they are not full-time) and retirement, as well as paid vacation days and holidays. But neither sick leave nor dental insurance is offered.

Moving From Contingent to Regular Employment

How does the contingent workforce relate to the regular workforce? The key point is that the contingent workforce is an entry port into the regular workforce. Job openings are posted internally; regular employees have the first chance, and reserve employees have the second chance at those jobs, before applicants from the external labor market are considered. Reserves purposefully constitute a recruiting pool and provide a screening function.

Some reserves are dismissed for unsatisfactory performance during an initial probation period (the figure was 17 percent in a recent year). After that, the low turnover rate of regular employees coupled with a modestly growing business means that it takes about three to four years for a reserve to become a regular employee. Reserves themselves turn over quite slowly (about 6 to 9 percent a year), and from 65 to 80 percent of them eventually become regular employees.

There are no moves in the opposite direction—regular employees do not become reserves. However, the company offers a small number of unpaid short-term leaves of absence to regular employees.

(See Sidebar 6-1 for a contrasting report of how contingent labor is managed in an Avon facility in Germany.)

▼▼▼

SIDEBAR 6-1

Using Contingent Workers in Germany: Experience of U.S. and German Operations of One Company

Companies in Europe need workforce flexibility and face cost pressures just like American companies do. They also use contingent labor, made up of temporary workers, part-time employees, and independent contractors. But European companies are likely to differ from their U.S. counterparts in how they use contingent workers. Especially in continental Europe, companies face different labor markets, different labor laws and regulations, and different institutions and customs from American companies. No western European country is more different from the United States in these respects than Germany. These differences mean that German companies use contingent labor in some distinctive ways from American companies.

To illustrate the German approach to using contingent labor, we look at a German facility of Avon Products that is similar in its functions and size to the U.S. East Coast facility described in this chapter. Both facilities are main distribution centers for consumer products located on the outskirts of large metropolitan areas, and both employ 800 to 1,000 people.

The German managers do two main things differently from the American managers in their use of contingent labor:

1. German managers hire short-term contract workers with a fixed work schedule for three- to six-month periods, in contrast to the American managers' practice of hiring employees who are on-call with an uncertain work schedule for an indefinite period. The German short-term contract employees can renew their contracts, staying with the company for one year or less in total, while the American on-call employees stay more than three years on the average.
2. German managers use fewer contingent workers than the American managers (even though the workload fluctuations they face are greater than at the American facility), but they tailor their use more closely to workload fluctuations.

Contingent workers amount to 10 percent of the German facility's head count on average, but 30 percent at the American counterpart; the range in the number of contingent workers at the German plant over a year is from 4 to 15 percent of head count while at the American location the range is from only 27 to 31 percent of head count. The German managers are able to use fewer contingent workers because they also get flexibility from their regular workforce, mainly via overtime hours.

Why do these differences show up, all in the same company? The answers come from differences in the labor markets faced by the two companies, and in differences in German and U.S. regulations and customs. The German facility faced a tight local labor market and could not get people to work on a contingent basis without the certainty of a contract. German federal law allows a maximum of $1\frac{1}{2}$ years as a contract employee at the same company. German contingent workers cannot stay for three years or more. Accordingly, German contingent workers do not see contingent working as a way in to regular employment to the same extent that American workers do. Many of the German contingent workers prefer to be contingent (30 to 40 percent by the company's estimates), whereas almost none of their American counterparts in this company do.

Premium pay for overtime hours is less in Germany, 25 percent as opposed to 50 percent, so it is cheaper to get flexibility from the regular workforce. By German law, contingent workers get the same benefits as core employees except for pension, and the benefits are noncontributory. There is no financial incentive to use contingent workers.

Lessons Learned

The contingent labor program at Avon works quite well, and has done so for many years. The company's objective—to manage the seasonal fluctuations in workload—is achieved. The company's flexibility need is an operational one, and it is met by contingent part-time employee staffing. It is a straightforward solution to a single problem. The workload in this fairly stable business fluctuates quite predictably over a relatively long cycle.

Contingent work at Avon is not a true core-ring setup, and the intent is not to create a buffer workforce for regular employees. Employment security is not an explicitly stated corporate goal. Contingent workers are not intended to be separate from regular employees. They are company people, they are employees, they do many of the same jobs as regular employees, they are paid the same wage rates as regular employees, they are entitled to several benefits, they are fairly long-serving, and most of them expect to become regular employees (and many do).

Avon is lucky, perhaps. The East Coast distribution facility is in a big labor market, and the supply of contingent workers exceeds the company's demand for them. Avon is regarded as a good employer. Avon appeals to women both by virtue of its business and its predominantly female management. Other big businesses in the area that hire large numbers of production workers include automobile assembly and chemical manufacturing companies, whose production jobs might not appeal as much to women. And Avon believes that it pays above-market wages.

The Avon contingent employees are not very different from the Avon regular employees; hence, managing them is not very different either. The contingent employees do not get all benefits, and they have some uncertainty about when and how much they will work. But the predictability of the workload fluctuations and the use of seniority to call in contingent employees minimizes the uncertainty.

Who Are the Contingent Workers?

As we've seen from the case examples in this and other chapters, some notable personal characteristics of contingent workers emerge.

To manage contingent workers so that they perform well and are treated well, we need to know something about who they are. What are their personal characteristics? What is their work background? Why are they contingent workers? Of course they are not a monolith, and it is dangerous to stereotype any category of workers because some individuals in the category will not fit the stereotype. Some U.S. data exist for the demographic characteristics of part-time and temporary workers, though not for other types of contingent workers such as independent contractors, and not all part-time workers are contingent. Nevertheless, some patterns emerge that are useful to know about.

Demographics: Age, Gender, Race, and Marital and Family Status

Part-time employees tend to be younger than full-time employees. For example, one-third of all part-timers are between the ages of 16 and 24 while less than half are in the prime working ages of 25 to 54. In contrast, only one-tenth of full-time employees are in the young age group while three-quarters are in the prime working ages. However, temporary workers are similar in age to full-time employees. (See Figure 6-1.)

Both part-time employees and temporary workers are much more likely to be women than full-time employees. Among full-timers, 45 percent are women; among part-timers, 67 percent are women, and among temporaries, 72 percent are women, as of 1993. (See Figure 6-2.) However, the numbers of temporaries who are men are growing especially rapidly.

There are essentially no differences in the racial makeup of full-time, part-time, and temporary workers—about 11 percent of each are blacks.

Both part-time and temporary workers are more likely to be single—51 percent of them are single—than full-time employees, only 37 percent of whom are single.[6] But there appears to be little difference in the number of these workers who have children. Just under half of temporaries, part-timers, and full-timers come from households with children. Putting these two pieces of information together tells us that part-time and temporary workers are more likely than full-time employees to be single parents.

Figure 6-1. Age of full-time, part-time, and temporary workers.

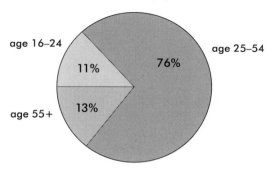

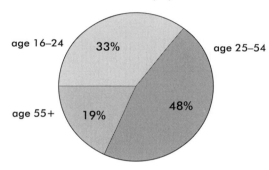

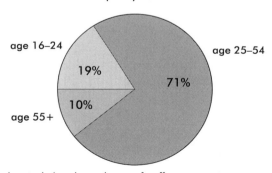

Note: Temporary workers include only employees of staffing companies.
Sources: For full-time and part-time employees: *Employment and Earnings,* U.S. Bureau of Labor Statistics, January 1994; for temporary workers: National Association of Temporary and Staffing Services, 1994.

Figure 6-2. Gender of full-time, part-time, and temporary workers.

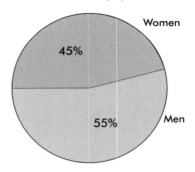

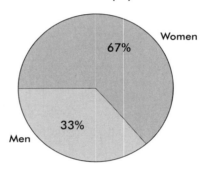

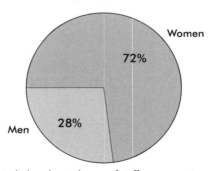

Note: Temporary workers include only employees of staffing companies.
Sources: Employment and Earnings, U.S. Bureau of Labor Statistics, January 1994; National Association of Temporary and Staffing Services, 1994.

Work Preparation:
Education, Training, and Experience

The education, training, and experience of part-time and temporary workers tell us about the qualifications they bring to the labor market.

Part-time employees have somewhat less education than full-time employees—fewer have completed college and more have stopped with a high school diploma. However, some of this difference comes from the larger number of part-timers who are young and who are adding to their formal education while they are employed part-time. Temporaries from staffing companies compare fairly closely to full-time employees in their educational qualifications. They are almost as likely to have a college degree as are full-time employees, and more temporaries than full-timers have some college or trade school education beyond high school. (See Figure 6-3.)

Contingent workers are unlikely to get as much training from the companies where they work as regular employees simply because they do not stay long enough for the company to recover its training investment. The training they do get will be skill training that applies directly to the job they do. Temporary workers get some training from the staffing companies that employ them. A survey done for the National Association of Temporary and Staffing Services reported that such employees got about 11 to 12 hours of skill training from their respective agencies in 1993. In the workforce as a whole, about 35 percent of all employed people get training once they are on the job in any given year (the figure comes from a 1990 book, *Training in America*, by Anthony Carnevale, Leila J. Gainer, and Janice Villet, published by Jossey-Bass).

Experience as a qualification for work is partly a matter of how much time a person spends working and partly a matter of what is done with that time. Contingent workers do not have the quantity of experience that regular employees have; they either work part-time or they work full-time but with interruptions (of course not all regular employees have continuous full-time work experience either). And because of their concentration in the less-skilled occupations, contingent workers do not have the quality of experience that regular employees have.

For the record, part-time employees work about 18 to 20 hours a

Figure 6-3. Education of full-time, part-time, and temporary workers.

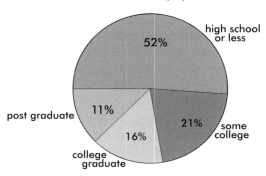

Full–Time Employees

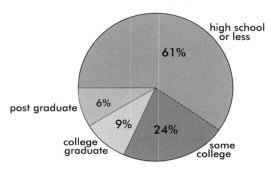

Part–Time Employees

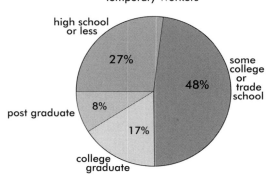

Temporary Workers

Notes: Data for full-time and part-time workers refer to age 16+. Part-time includes workers who prefer part-time employment as well as those who would rather work full-time. Data for temporaries refer to employees of staffing companies.
Sources: Current Population Survey unpublished data and National Association of Temporary and Staffing Services.

week and about 31 weeks per year on the average—altogether amounting to only 620 hours a year, or about one-third as much as full-time year-round work.[7] Among temporaries from staffing companies, roughly half are between regular jobs; for these people, temporary work is a bridge from one job to another, and their work experience might be no different from that of a core employee. They expect to be a temporary only a few months. The other half of temporary workers choose this type of work for other reasons—family and personal—and their work experience is likely to be less than that of regular employees.[8]

The Resources and Choices of Contingent Workers

How do contingent workers differ from core employees in the resources they bring to the labor market? In regard to their personal characteristics, they are more likely to be women. Part-timers in particular are younger. In their work preparation, contingent workers cannot expect to get as much training or experience as regular employees. Part-timers in particular have less education. Both part-timers and temporaries are concentrated in less-skilled, lower-paying occupations.

Clearly many such workers have less human capital and bring fewer resources and less personal power to the labor market than regular employees. These workers appear to be no less dependent than regular employees on income from their work for their economic well-being. While this applies to the part-timers and temporaries for which we have data, the situation of highly specialized technical and professional contingent workers who are independent contractors may be radically different. The characteristics of these types of workers are not revealed by government statistics on self-employed workers because many self-employed workers are not contingent workers.

How many contingent workers choose to be contingent? What range of choice do they really have? The answer cannot be given simply as one figure because people's choices depend on the alternatives that they have. If wages and benefits are much better in core employment, then not so many people will choose contingent work. If there is no job available in the core, then contingent work begins to look better. Some people intrinsically prefer contingent work and do it indefinitely if they can. One manager described such a case:

> The people who really are true to their professions, they prefer contingent work. . . . My husband is one of those—he doesn't want anything to do with the corporate world, he just doesn't like bureaucracies. As long as I am the full-time core employee and able to get benefits, then it's okay that he's a contingent worker.

In the nation as a whole, among the part-timers in the labor force who are contingent workers, an educated guess is that somewhat less than 60 percent prefer to be contingent; they are the voluntary part-time contingent employees. Among temporaries from staffing companies, somewhat less than half choose to be temporaries as a preferred way of working and do not want to shift to regular full-time or part-time employment. They want to be temporaries indefinitely, for a variety of reasons—they need time with their families, they want to pursue other interests, they feel less stress as temporaries, they like the diversity of working on different assignments, or they want flexibility in work time. These include people who have been offered full-time positions by their client companies but turned it down because they wanted to remain temporary workers. (See Table 6-1.) Other people who are temporaries only "choose" it instrumentally—they use it as a way to get a regular job—and they do not expect to be a temporary worker for more than a few weeks or months.

The experience of managers reinforces the belief that roughly only half of all contingent workers freely choose this work arrangement. Hewlett-Packard was unable to find enough people to be contingent-by-choice so that it could operate a separate core-ring flexibility model. In another company, one manager put it this way: "We find that for the most part our contingent workers want to come into the organization as a stepping-stone to go full-time or get a regular part-time position, and they don't really want temporary work."

The picture we see of contingent workers is that they are people who are on the average less well-equipped for the world of work than regular employees, and many of them (maybe half or more) do not really want to be contingent workers. Many independent contractors are probably an exception to this generalization, although data are

Table 6-1. Who works as a temporary employee and why.

Reason for Temporary Work	How Many?	Personal Characteristics—likely to be:
"Between jobs"	39%	Sole income earner, well-educated, shortest time as a temporary
"Skill builders"	14%	Younger worker, less educated than other temporaries
"Choose to temp"	10%	Older woman, second income earner, longest time as a temporary
"Parents"	8%	Woman with children
Not strongly identified with any category	29%	Not applicable

Notes: The categories were created by a factor analysis of survey responses from temporaries in staffing companies in 1993; the labels for the categories were chosen by the study's author.
Source: Bruce Steinberg, "Temporary Workforce Profile 1994," *Contemporary Times,* Summer 1994.

lacking. The management of contingent workers—focusing on obtaining cost-effective performance from them—cannot ignore their socioeconomic status.

Paying Contingent Workers

One of the main decisions in managing contingent workers is how much to pay them in wages and benefits, and how to deliver the payment.

How and how much a company pays contingent workers is one ingredient in determining how cost-effective they are. It affects the amount of cash paid out, and it might also affect how well these employees work and how long they stay. In addition, wages and benefits are a very visible point of comparison between contingent workers and core employees, with transparent equity consequences.

Wages—How Much to Pay

In the United States overall, contingent workers are paid less than regular employees. Hourly-paid part-time employees get one-third less than hourly-paid full-time employees on the average, and temporary workers get one-quarter less (see Figure 6-4, which shows median wages for workers paid on an hourly basis). None of these data include independent contractors who are contingent workers.

Averages conceal as much as they reveal. Some of the wage gap comes about because contingent workers are concentrated in lower-paying occupations. For example, agency temporaries who are in top-end professional specialty jobs actually earn more than full-time employees while temporaries who are machine operators or laborers at the bottom of the occupational distribution make scarcely half as much as their full-time counterparts (see Table 6-2).

We don't expect average wages of contingent workers to equal those of regular employees. Contingent workers typically are

Figure 6-4. Wages of full-time, part-time, and temporary workers.

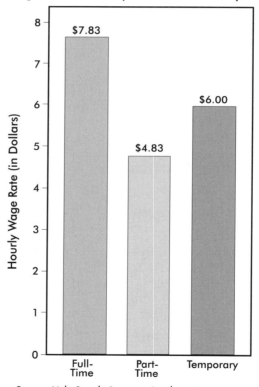

Sources: *Industry Wage Survey: Help Supply Services,* October 1989, U.S. Bureau of Labor Statistics, 1993, and Thomas Nardone, "Contingent Workers: Characteristics and Trends," unpublished, 1993.

Table 6-2. Hourly wages of temporary and full-time workers in major occupations.

Wage Measure and Occupation	Full-Timers	Temporaries	Difference for Temporaries
Hourly earnings by occupation, 1989			
All occupations	$11.50*	$ 7.59	− 34%
Professional specialty	16.89*	22.14	+ 31
Administrative and clerical	9.54*	7.30	− 24
Service occupations	7.29*	5.70	− 22
Operators and laborers	9.31*	5.15	− 45

Note: Temporaries refers only to employees of staffing companies who work at client firms.
*Indicates figures are estimated by the authors from data on weekly earnings and average hours worked per week; the full-time workers are wage and salary workers. Temporaries' salaries represent an average wage; full-timers' salaries represent a median wage. Average wages are higher than median wages because the distribution is skewed upward, so figures for temporary workers are biased upward in the comparison with full-time workers. Because the data services and data collection methods for full-timers and temporaries differ, comparisons between the two may be subject to unknown distortions.
Sources: U.S. Bureau of Labor Statistics, *Industry Wage Survey: Help Supply Services, October 1989,* Bulletin 2430, September 1993; and U.S. Bureau of Labor Statistics, *Employment and Earnings,* vol. 37, no. 1, January 1990.

younger and have less education or training or workforce experience, and less time on their current job than regular employees. The supply of contingent workers appears to be ample, and they are less likely to be represented by labor unions than hourly-paid production workers. They do not have as much power in the labor market as regular employees.

Inside work units in companies, we find different pay scenarios for contingent workers. In some cases they are paid less than regular employees who do similar jobs; in many cases they are paid the same wage rate, as at Avon; in a very few cases they are paid a little more, as at Hewlett-Packard—to make up for some of the benefits they do not get.

Wages—How to Pay Them

Should contingent workers get raises? Should merit be a criterion? Sometimes this question does not arise because contingent workers stay at one company for only a short time, so they are paid a fixed wage rate for that period. But in other cases, managers want contingent workers to stay longer, and so wage increases can be used to induce the contingent worker to continue. For example, a wage increase might be offered at four or six months of service. Or, acknowledging the likelihood that a contingent worker's productivity will go up with a little experience on the job, a merit pay raise might be offered to those contingent workers whose performance is above average. If the base wage rate is low, the percentage increase will need to be quite large to be effective, but it will be worth it for the company if the worker's output really exceeds the average.

Benefits

Nationwide, the benefits picture for contingent workers is very simple: Few get any. No one is surprised to know this because for many companies it is the avoidance of benefits, both the money and the trouble, that is a key attraction of contingent workers. Look at statistics for just two main benefits, paid vacation time and health insurance. Among full-time employees, about 80 percent get paid vacation; only about 25 percent of part-time employees get this benefit, and only about 10 percent of temporaries from staffing companies get it. Health insurance that is at least partly paid for by the employer is received by 72 percent of full-time employees, but only by 15 percent of part-time employees and maybe 1 percent of agency temporaries. (See Figure 6-5.)

One reason why contingent workers do not get benefits is that they do not stay with a company long enough. This is especially true for temporaries with staffing companies. Paid vacation is available to almost three-quarters of these temporaries—the staffing company offers the benefit. But the benefit can only be taken up if the temporary employee fulfills a length of service requirement. For more than half of these temporaries, at least nine months of service is required before the paid vacation benefit can be received. Table 6-3 indicates how many contingent workers are able to take advantage of various benefits.

Designing a Compensation Package

Managers' choices about how to handle wages and benefits for contingent workers can follow two basic guidelines. First, what matters

Figure 6-5. Benefits for full-time, part-time, and temporary workers.

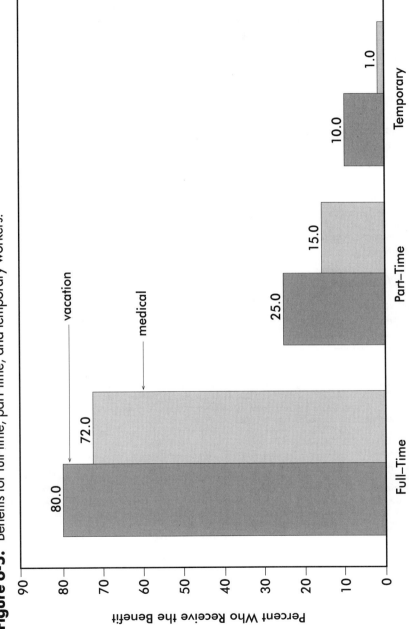

Sources: U.S. Bureau of Labor Statistics reports: *Industry Wage Survey: Help Supply Services,* October 1989; *Employee Benefits in Medium and Large Firms,* 1989; and Thomas Nardone, "Contingent Workers: Characteristics and Trends," unpublished, 1993.

Table 6-3. Benefits for temporary, part-time, and full-time workers (1989).

Benefit	Temporaries	Part-Timers	Full-Timers: Big Companies	Full-Timers: Small Companies
Paid Vacation				
Available to:	74%	37%	97%	88%
Received by:	10	15–30*	80–90*	70–80*
Paid Holidays				
Available to:	56	35	97	84
Received by:	23	na	na	na
Life Insurance				
Available to:	38	18	94	64
All employer-paid for:	4	14	82	53
Received by:	1	na	na	na
Health Insurance				
Available to:	51	17	92	69
All employer-paid for:	3	10	48	40
Received by:	1	15	——— 72 ———	

*These figures are the authors' estimates based on length of service requirements.
Notes: "Temporaries" refers only to employees of staffing companies who work at client firms. Data for part-time workers refer to 1990–1991. Big company means 100 or more employees; small company means less than 100 employees. "Available to" means that the employer provides the benefit. "Received by" means that the employee actually was able to use the benefit. "All employer-paid" means that the employer paid all costs of the benefit.
Sources: U.S. Bureau of Labor Statistics reports: *Industy Wage Survey: Help Supply Services, October 1989,* Bulletin 2430, September 1993; *Employee Benefits in Medium and Large Firms 1989,* Bulletin 2363, June 1990; *Employee Benefits in Small Private Establishments 1990,* Bulletin 2388, September 1991; and *BLS Reports on Employee Benefits in the United States 1990–91,* June 1993. More recent data for full-time and part-time workers are available in *Employee Benefits in Medium and Large Establishments 1991,* Bulletin 2422, May 1993; *Employee Benefits in Small Private Establishments 1992,* Bulletin 2441, May 1994; and *Employee Benefits in the United States 1991–92,* June 1994. For data on health insurance benefits for part-timers, see Thomas J. Nardone, "Contingent Workers: Characteristics and Trends," unpublished paper, 1993.

is the sum of both wages and benefits, or total compensation. Second, to manage contingent workers well requires equity but not equality with core employees.

Start with benefits. Some contingent workers do not need costly benefits like health insurance because their spouse or domestic partner has coverage from his or her employer (this is equally true, in fact more true, of core employees, but this fact does not alter the argument). Other contingent workers do not want benefits—for example, 20-year-old college students hardly care to participate in a retirement plan in which they will never be vested. Therefore, the interests of the contingent workers themselves are not harmed by lack of some benefits. Respond fairly to individual needs that differ from worker to worker.

If contingent workers are employees of your company and work less than full-time hours over the course of a year, one approach to compensation is to offer them some benefits, such as leave time for vacation or holidays or personal time, prorated to the amount of time they work, and to skip other benefits that are hard to prorate or less desired by the contingent workers. Such an equitable approach is easier to implement if your company has a flexible benefits plan that allows the workers themselves a range of choice about which benefits they receive.

An alternative approach is to skip all benefits for contingent workers and instead pay them a wage premium as a partial substitute. The wage premium does not need to equal the value of foregone benefits if the contingent workers, who tend to be younger than regular employees, place higher value on current income than deferred income. The trade-off between wage premium and benefits can be tailored to the local labor market.

If contingent workers are not employees of the company where they work but instead are supplied by a staffing or leasing company or are independent contractors, then the client company has no benefits decision to make. The decision is which staffing company to use, and what fee to pay. How much compensation is received by the contingent workers is still of interest to the client company, however. A situation in which temporaries get less pay than core employees and few or no benefits may be a prelude to shaky performance and may not be in anyone's best interests.

Do Contingent Workers Become Core Employees?

One of the most important and vexing sets of questions in managing contingent workers is this: Do contingent workers move into regular employment? Is the contingent workforce a screen or "proving ground" for future core employees and in part a recruiting device? This is the Avon approach. Or is the contingent workforce really separate, with little or no mobility across the core-contingent boundary? This is the Hewlett-Packard approach.

To decide, first ask: What is the objective? Do you want contingent workers to move into regular employment, or do you want to keep the two workforces separate?

Why and How to Keep Them Separate

An impermeable boundary between core and contingent workforces is an appealing idea, for two reasons:

1. *Equity reasons*—Contingent workers are different in status from regular employees in most people's eyes, so you want contingent workers to be people who prefer and willfully choose this type of work.
2. *Legal reasons*—Potential exposure to legal problems coming from contingent workers is minimized if they are as separate as possible from the regular workforce (see Chapter 7 for more discussion of legal aspects).

The downside of separated core and contingent workforces with no movement between them is that it is hard to do successfully, as Hewlett-Packard discovered. Consider a few preconditions and a few guidelines, any one of which if present or followed improves the chances for success (they don't all have to hold):

- Use temporaries from a staffing company or independent contractors as your contingent workers rather than making them employees on your payroll. It is difficult to manage two classes of employees who are separate but unequal.
- Do not let contingent workers do the same jobs as regular employees in the same work unit for very long.

- Provide an equitable if not equal compensation package to that received by regular employees. If regular employment is more attractive financially, more contingent workers will prefer it.
- Do not keep the same contingent workers on the job in the company for long time periods. The longer they stay the more they become like regular employees.
- Examine corporate culture—an emphasis on inclusiveness and teamwork is at odds with a contingent workforce that is separate in status without mobility into the core; your managers will feel this as much as your contingent workers.
- Assess your labor market. Make sure that it is big and contains lots of people who are likely to prefer contingent worker status, such as students, retirees, and second income earners.

Practically speaking, no matter what the company's policy is, what some operating managers will want to do in their work units is to hire the best person they can get when they have a job opening, and this person might be a contingent worker in that unit whom they have personally observed. Even if the guidelines and preconditions are in place, the core-contingent separation will be hard to enforce because managers don't like to let opportunities to take demonstrated excellent contingent workers into the core slip away.

Why and How to Go for Mobility

Taking contingent workers into regular employment is an appealing idea for three reasons:

1. You are more likely to get an employee who is a good performer without putting out high recruiting and selection costs. You have observed this employee amid lots of contingent workers in the company, and you know something about his or her work habits and abilities. The company operates an internal labor market. The contingent workforce is the entry port. Screening occurs there while the company's flexibility need is being met.
2. If contingent workers know they are competing for a slot in the core workforce, they are motivated to do their best as contingent workers.
3. Because many managers want to recruit new core employees

from the contingent workforce, a policy of doing so is simply in harmony with preferred practice.

To successfully follow a policy of moving contingent workers into core employment, consider the four guidelines that follow:

1. Provide equitable pay, benefits, and privileges of employment to contingent workers. You want to attract good people into the contingent workforce, and you don't want future core employees to begin their association with you as second-class citizens.
2. Take a reasonable number of contingent workers into regular employment, as a share of those who look for this mobility, within a time period that you and they see as reasonable. You don't want contingent workers with frustrated expectations, or workers who quit before you convert them to regular employee status.
3. Use similar employment qualifications for recruiting contingent workers as for core employees so that they can compete fairly for core job openings when they occur.
4. Keep the external recruiting and selection function alive and well. Passive reliance on selection from contingent workers might leave you with an overly narrow slice of workforce opportunities, and it can make managers lazy if all they have to do is watch contingent workers.

Endnotes

1. This is what Tom Kochan and others found in a case study of safety problems in a petrochemical plant. See Kochan, Thomas A., et al., "Human Resource Strategies and Contingent Workers: The Case of Safety and Health in the Petrochemical Industry," *Human Resources Management*, vol. 33, no. 1 (Spring 1994).
2. This case was prepared by the first author and is based on discussions with several human resources executives and operating managers at corporate headquarters and at one manufacturing plant. I am grateful for the cooperation of the company officials, especially Tom Pierson. Errors of fact remain my responsibility, and interpretations are my own.
3. Of course, achieving flexibility by matching closely the amount of labor

needed also saves costs compared either to paying lots of overtime or having idle workers.

4. To take such a position on cost is easier for HP than for some other companies because HP is not a labor-intensive company.

5. This case was prepared by the first author and is based on discussions with several human resources executives and operating managers at corporate headquarters and at four manufacturing and distribution facilities, one of which is referred to in this case. I am grateful for the cooperation of the company officials. Errors of fact remain my responsibility, and interpretations are my own.

6. These numbers refer to 1989 and are obtained from the January 1990 issue of *Employment and Earnings,* the monthly book of statistics published by the U.S. Bureau of Labor Statistics, and from surveys of temporaries at staffing companies by the National Association of Temporary and Staffing Services in Alexandria, Virginia.

7. These data come from statistics published by the U.S. Bureau of Labor Statistics, some of which are summarized in Nollen, Stanley D., Eddy, Brenda Broz, and Martin, Virginia Hider, *Permanent Part-Time Employment: The Manager's Perspective* (New York: Praeger, 1978).

8. These data and those which follow come from survey research done by the National Association of Temporary and Staffing Services (NATSS) in Alexandria, Virginia. They are published in the NATSS journal, *Contemporary Times* (Spring 1994).

7

Weighing the Legal Considerations

by Jeffrey S. Klein

As a cost saving measure, Eastman Kodak Company out-sourced a group of employees to Digital Equipment Corporation and then contracted for their continued services. When Digital Equipment terminated the employment of two such employees, they each sued Kodak and Digital Equipment for $10 million in punitive damages, alleging breach of fiduciary duty under ERISA regarding their benefits, and misrepresentation regarding the details of employment with Digital Equipment.[1]

Quicksilver Messenger Service has battled the Illinois Department of Employment Security and the IRS for five years in challenging the reclassification of its messengers as employees, rather than independent contractors. Penalties, assessed back taxes, and professional fees to fight the

Jeffrey S. Klein is a partner in the Employment Law and ERISA Department at Weil, Gotshal & Manges, a domestic and international commercial law firm. Mr. Klein received his J.D. from Columbia University Law School, is the author of articles on employment law and litigation, and writes a bimonthly column for the *New York Law Journal* concerning current developments in employment law. He is an authority on contingent employment issues and lectures to corporate legal departments and human resources managers on the implementation and management of alternative staffing arrangements. Nancy Y. Tong, an associate of the firm, assisted in the preparation of this chapter.

reclassification have already cost the company upwards of $100,000, with more to come when overtime pay owed the reclassified employees is calculated. All this for a company that uses about 100 messengers![2]

This chapter explores the legal issues that define—or should define—the way companies manage their contingent workers. As Eastman Kodak Company and Quicksilver Messenger Service belatedly have realized, the legal costs associated with contingent workers were more than they had bargained for. Yet many companies assume that a contingent workforce always reduces the legal obligations inherent in the conventional employer-employee relationship. Many also do not realize that when a staffing firm is involved, legal obligations may become *more* complicated, not less. Under these circumstances, the company and staffing firm—as "joint employers" or "co-employers"—each may have actual or potential legal duties of an employer toward those workers.

The purpose of this chapter is to identify the significant legal issues that remain, or are created, when contingent staffing arrangements are chosen. The message of this chapter is simple: In developing a strategic plan for using contingent workers, you must reconcile any differences that may exist between your perceptions about contingent work relationships and the realities of those relationships in the eyes of the law. You must be knowledgeable about your legal obligations—and the common pitfalls you may encounter—even when you consciously choose to have another firm serve as the "employer" of record or believe you have distanced yourself from workers whom you consider to be "independent contractors." In the end, you may find that, due to the attendant legal risks, using contingent workers gives your company less of an advantage than you had expected.

You and Your Contingent Workers— Defining the Relationship

The starting point in evaluating your legal obligations is understanding the nature of your relationship to the contingent workers. In general, legal duties and obligations arise when an employer-employee relationship exists between the parties.

What Are the Determining Factors?

The law classifies your contingent workers either as employees—when there is an employment relationship—or as independent contractors—when there is not—based on an evaluation of all the facts and circumstances of that work relationship. The classification of a contingent worker as either an employee or independent contractor depends upon whether you have a right to control the terms and conditions of employment, whether or not such control is exercised. This determination is based upon factors derived from the common law, which have been memorialized by the IRS with respect to tax matters and are commonly known as the "20-factors" test, set forth in Figure 7-1.

The existence of sufficient control suggests an employee status while the absence of such control suggests an independent contractor status. Thus, a contingent worker will be considered an employee if you have the right to specify the timing, duration, sequence, hours, and location of the work to be done. By contrast, the worker likely will be considered an independent contractor if such worker has a finite rather than a continuous work relationship with your company, possesses special skills not available in your company's core workforce, provides services to others, or shows other evidence of an independent business operation.

The common law "right to control" test provides the narrowest definition of an employer-employee relationship. However, other, more expansive approaches in defining an employer-employee relationship are used in different contexts, including civil rights, wage and hour, and labor relations. The broadest approach, known as the "economic realities" test, asks whether the worker is economically dependent for his or her livelihood on the company for which he or she performs services. In fact, in 1994 the Dunlop Commission (formally known as the Commission on the Future of Worker-Management Relations) recommended the adoption of the economic realities test in applying labor, employment, and tax laws to contingent staffing arrangements.[3] If such a change is implemented, the scope of employer liability under those laws would likely expand.

Why Staffing Arrangements Matter

The type of contingent workers you choose to supplement your core workforce depends on the needs of your company. (See Chapter 2.)

Figure 7-1. The 20-factors test: Who is an employee?

The IRS has identified 20 factors derived from the common law to indicate whether sufficient control exists to establish an employer-employee relationship. These factors serve only as guides—the degree of importance of each factor depends on occupation and context. In general, workers who are considered employees can be expected to:

1. Comply with instructions about when, where, and how work is done
2. Receive on-the-job training or formal instruction
3. Perform services that are integrated into business operations
4. Render services personally
5. Rely on the employer to hire, supervise, and pay assistants
6. Maintain a continuing relationship with the business where services are performed
7. Comply with set hours of work
8. Devote full time to the business
9. Work on the employer's premises or in locations sanctioned or required by the employer
10. Perform services in a set order or sequence
11. Submit oral or written reports
12. Receive payment by salary or time, not by job or commission
13. Receive reimbursement for business and/or traveling expenses
14. Look to the employer to furnish tools, materials, and equipment
15. Lack significant investment in the business
16. Realize no profit or loss from work performed
17. Work for one company at a time
18. Not make services available to the general public
19. Be subject to discharge at will by the employer
20. Have the right to terminate the employment relationship at any time

Source: Rev. Rul. 87-41, 1987-1 C.B. 296.

But beyond matching a particular type of staffing arrangement to your individual needs, each such arrangement can be viewed along an employee/independent contractor continuum, depending on the degree of control you have.

On-Call Part-Time and Direct-Hire Temporaries

On-call part-time and direct-hire temporary workers (including workers belonging to an in-house temporary pool) are your employees. Although such part-timers and temps may work only when needed on short-term, finite projects or may be placed on a payroll separate from your core workforce, you generally maintain control over hiring, training, discipline, supervision, and direction. Perhaps the most significant area distinguishing these contingent workers from your core employees is benefits eligibility, which we will examine later in this chapter.

Temporary Help, Outsourcing, and Leasing

Temporary help, outsourcing, and leasing are contingent staffing arrangements involving a third party, which we refer to collectively in this chapter as "staffing firms." Staffing firms also frequently identify themselves as "professional employers." A temporary help arrangement refers to contingent workers hired by a staffing firm and assigned to your company to support or supplement the workforce in special work situations, such as employee absences, temporary skill shortages, seasonal workloads, and special projects. Outsourcing is an arrangement by which your company contracts out, and a third-party firm assumes responsibility for a particular function, with the workers performing such function being employed by the firm. For reasons that are discussed later regarding benefits and workers' compensation coverage, leasing traditionally has meant the transfer of the entire workforce to a leasing firm and lease-back of the same workforce. However, the modern definition of leasing more frequently encompasses a contractual arrangement whereby employment responsibilities are shared between your company and the leasing firm, which may entail staffing for certain job functions, a discrete department, or an entire workforce.

These temporary workers, outsourced workers, and leased employees are generally employees of those firms, not yours. As the employer of record, those firms are typically responsible for recruiting, hiring, and paying their employees, as well as managing human resources. In many situations, however, your company may also be regarded as a joint employer since the day-to-day management and supervision of such contingent workers (including, perhaps, some on-site training) remains under your control. (See "Joint Employer Status" later in this chapter.)

Independent Contractors

Independent contractors (also known as consultants or freelancers) theoretically have no employer-employee relationship with the companies for whom they perform services. By *theoretically*, we mean that if you use independent contractors who are properly classified as such, you have little or no control over how they do their work. They have a contractual obligation to perform certain services within a specified time frame for which they are paid a fee. Independent contractors are typically expected to maintain their own business and to be available to work for more than one client. Because they are not employees, they are usually excluded from benefit plans.

Determining who is and who is not an independent contractor has caused considerable confusion in recent years because many individuals who are classified as independent contractors by the companies that use their services are in fact as closely managed as regular employees of those companies. Sometimes the so-called independent contractors are retirees or former employees who were victims of downsizing or other restructuring measures, only to be brought back, "off the payroll."

We use the term "independent contractor" in this context to describe workers whom you hire directly. In addition, contingent workers supplied by a staffing firm who are employees of that firm may also be considered to have an independent contractor relationship to you.

Joint Employer Status

When contingent workers supplied by a staffing firm (i.e., third party) are working on your company's premises, it is quite likely that the staffing firm and your company are joint employers. As a result, you may find yourself liable as an employer to those workers. In most cases, this relationship arises because your company maintains control over the work by specifying the tasks to be done and by providing the day-to-day supervision of the workers. For example, you would be particularly vulnerable to incurring such liability when you allow the same "temporary" workers to remain on the job over long periods of time.

Joint employer liability is based on the actual allocation of employer responsibilities. Generally, your company cannot avoid joint employer status merely by applying a legal label to your staffing arrangement. Rather, joint employer status will exist when you have a right to control the activities of the contingent workers. As a joint employer, you are liable when you violate the law, or when you fail to act when you become aware of a possible violation. You also may be liable when the staffing firm fails to meet its part of the employer responsibilities but you take no action despite your knowledge of such failure.

Your liability as a joint employer largely depends on how you structure and implement the staffing arrangement. The more you are willing to cede control, the less likely you will be considered a joint employer. Figure 7-2 lists a series of questions that will help you assess how much control your company maintains over its contingent workers. The questions also may suggest areas in which control may

Figure 7-2. How much control do you have over your contingent workers?

1. *Do you control or have the right to control:*
   - Recruiting and screening policies and procedures?
   - Hiring criteria and decisions?
   - Titles and job descriptions?
   - Training?
   - Assignment or supervision of work, shifts, hours of service, and additional projects?
   - Payment of compensation?
   - Benefits and leave policies?
2. *Do you establish or have the right to establish:*
   - Pay rates?
   - Office policies and procedures?
   - Manner in which work is performed?
   - Promotions or transfers?
3. *Have you reserved the right to:*
   - Discipline?
   - Transfer?
   - Promote?
   - Discharge?
   - Request a replacement worker if you receive unsatisfactory service?
4. *Have you specified in the written agreement with the staffing firm that contingent workers supplied under the agreement are independent contractors?*

be more or less important to your company, allowing you to minimize your risks by restructuring your contingent worker arrangements.

Legal Issues—How Your Company Is Affected

Once you have determined whether or not an employer-employee
relationship exists between your company and the contingent workers, you can proceed to evaluate the legal responsibilities you have
toward these workers. The following sections illustrate some of the
legal issues that may arise when your company uses contingent
staffing arrangements.

Employment Taxes

Perhaps the area posing the greatest risk for companies is the misclassification of workers as independent contractors, resulting in costly
penalties imposed by the IRS for failure to pay employment taxes.
Companies are frequently enticed by the significant tax savings associated with classifying workers as independent contractors—even
when such workers do not meet the common law criteria. In doing
so, companies do not pay the employer's share of social security taxes
under FICA (Federal Income Contributions Act) and unemployment
taxes under FUTA (Federal Unemployment Tax Act), nor do they
withhold and pay over income taxes to the IRS. Instead, independent
contractors are responsible for the payment of social security taxes
and must make quarterly estimated income tax payments. In addition, independent contractors are not covered by workers' compensation, unemployment insurance, and other benefit protections that
employees enjoy.

Companies may bear heavy costs when their independent contractors are reclassified as employees. Upon reclassification, a company is required to reimburse the government for all the taxes that
should have been paid—its share of social security and unemployment taxes, the employee's share of social security taxes, employee
income tax withholding, state taxes, and the accumulated interest on
these taxes. The company also may be subject to civil penalties. This
employment tax liability is reduced if the company previously filed

1099 forms for its independent contractors who subsequently are re-classified as employees and did not intentionally disregard withholding obligations. However, failure to file 1099 forms consistent with claimed independent contractor status may result in a doubling of the liability.[4]

The proliferation of independent contractors whose compensation is not subject to withholding for taxes often means lost tax revenue to the government—a major reason for the IRS's heightened interest in independent contractors. In 1996, misclassification is expected to result in $2.1 billion in lost federal revenues.[5]

Another reason for IRS scrutiny is the practice of bringing back former employees as independent contractors following successive waves of corporate downsizing, thus allowing companies to replace lost talent while complying with head count restrictions. These workers often continue to do the same jobs they performed as employees, but no longer have taxes withheld from their paychecks.

The IRS is also paying close attention to industries where significant numbers of independent contractors are found. Industries and occupations of particular interest include young, fast-growing businesses, engineering and high-tech companies, so-called temp-intensive industries (such as publishing, entertainment, advertising, telecommunications, software, and construction), and certain jobs such as sales representatives and drivers.[6]

The perceived abuses of misclassifying employees as independent contractors also have been the target of legislative initiatives—including, for example, the Contingent Workforce Equity Act.[7] This piece of legislation, which was introduced in the 103d Congress in 1994, would have shifted the burden of proof more heavily toward the employer to demonstrate independent contractor status.

Safe-Harbor Provision

A safe-harbor provision, Section 530 of the Revenue Act of 1978, provides protection to companies which may have classified their workers as independent contractors. In order to fall within this safe-harbor protection, a company must demonstrate that (1) the workers were not treated as employees in the past, (2) the company filed federal tax returns consistent with nonemployee status, (3) a reasonable basis exists for treating the workers as independent contractors, and

(4) other individuals holding substantially similar positions were not treated as employees for purposes of employment taxes.[8]

"Reasonable basis" means judicial precedent or other ruling, a past IRS audit that resulted in no employment tax liability, or a long-standing practice or industry standard. Thus, companies in which regular employees do the same jobs as workers classified as independent contractors cannot rely on the safe harbor, but must make a more rigorous showing under the 20-factors test. Although companies could once expect the IRS to interpret the safe harbor liberally, considerably fewer requests for relief are now being granted.[9]

The Tax Reform Act of 1986 added a new Section 530(d) that limits the applicability of the safe harbor. More specifically, the safe harbor does not apply to technical service workers—engineers, designers, drafters, computer programmers, systems analysts, or others—who are supplied by a *third party* such as a staffing firm.[10] Instead, these workers must be evaluated under the common law rules. The safe-harbor provision would continue to apply, however, to direct-hire technical service workers.

If workers whom you classify as independent contractors are not covered by the Section 530 safe harbor, you can still avoid unintended conversion to employee status by making sure that they work without close supervision and are permitted to structure the way they complete their tasks. You can also formally document the intended independent contractor relationship in a contract. Guidelines for demonstrating such a relationship with your workers are provided in Figure 7-3.

Staffing Firm Role

What are your employment tax obligations if you use contingent workers supplied by a staffing firm? The general rule is that whoever controls the wage payments is the employer responsible for making the proper withholding, even though a joint employer relationship may exist between the client company and staffing firm.

General Motors v. United States illustrates the point. General Motors brought in design engineers who were supplied by a staffing firm and paid the staffing firm a fee for services rendered under the contract.[11] General Motors was unaware of the amount of wages and benefits paid to the engineers. When the staffing firm failed to remit employment taxes

Figure 7-3. How you can document an independent contractor relationship.

1. File Form 1099.
2. Execute a written agreement that reflects the following:
   - Specifies intent to treat the worker as an independent contractor.
   - Does not use the terms "employer" to refer to your company or "employee" to refer to the worker.
   - Avoids words and phrases to reflect your control over the work to be performed.
   - Describes a discrete job of finite duration.
   - Does not provide for termination before completion of the contract unless the worker fails to meet the contractual obligations.
   - Does not provide for reimbursement of expenses.
   - Requires the worker to cover any employees under workers' compensation insurance.
   - Provides for indemnification in the event that the worker is reclassified as an employee.
3. Retain copies of business cards, classified ads, and other documentation demonstrating that the worker is available to perform services for others.

for these workers, the IRS sought to collect the amount owed from General Motors.

The IRS argued that the staffing firm was no more than a disbursing agent and that General Motors was the employer since it exercised significant control over the engineers. The court determined, however, that the staffing firm, which controlled the wage payments, was responsible for withholding the employment taxes. Accordingly, no other party was in a position to make proper accounting for and payment of the employment taxes.[12]

Benefits

Contingent workers also raise issues about employee benefits. The areas discussed in this section are misclassifying employees as independent contractors, interfering with part-timers' eligibility for benefits, and using contingent workers supplied by a staffing firm on a long-term basis.

Independent Contractors

Daughtrey v. Honeywell demonstrates the risk of relying solely on the existence of a contract to prove an independent contractor status.[13] If you "flip" your employees to independent contractors, changing only the label and not the essence of the relationship, you may find yourself obligated to provide benefits to them because they remain your common law employees.

Jimmy Ruth Daughtrey, who had been laid off from her job at Honeywell as a computer programmer, was subsequently rehired as a consultant to work on a computer development project at the company under the supervision of a Honeywell representative. Honeywell provided all equipment and supplies, and required compliance with all company standards and operating procedures. Her consultant agreement designated her as an independent contractor having no rights to any benefits provided to Honeywell employees. When the project on which Daughtrey was working was discontinued and Honeywell terminated the consultant agreement, Daughtrey sued. One of her claims was brought under ERISA, seeking welfare and pension benefits for the period during which she was employed as a consultant.

Although the district court, relying on the consultant agreement, held that Daughtrey was an independent contractor not entitled to any benefits, the appellate court reinstated her claim, reasoning that Daughtrey was entitled to claim the status of a common law employee. The court found a number of elements in her relationship with Honeywell suggesting that she was an employee, including the fact that Honeywell furnished equipment and supplies, she was required to work at Honeywell's facilities, she was paid an hourly wage, she did not work for other clients, and she reported daily to a Honeywell supervisor.

Part-Time Employees

Another problem arises if you distinguish part-timers from full-time employees for the purposes of benefits entitlement. Section 510 of ERISA prohibits a company from interfering with an employee's attainment of any right to which the employee may become entitled under an employee benefit plan.[14] The case law in this area is sparse.

Certain standards, however, can guide your actions in administering your benefits plans.

An employer may cover full-time employees and exclude part-time employees who otherwise do not meet the minimum participation standards[15] under its benefit plans without violating Section 510. In *Rush v. McDonald's Corporation*, a part-time employee claimed that McDonald's had violated Section 510 by not providing her with the benefits of a full-time employee, although she performed the duties of a full-time employee.[16] The court rejected her claim, stating that ERISA did not bar employers from distinguishing between full-timers and part-timers for benefits purposes.

However, an employer who intentionally prevents a part-time employee from becoming a full-time employee to avoid covering that worker under its benefits plan may violate Section 510. In *Fleming v. Avers & Associates*, an employer actually discharged a part-time employee in order to avoid incurring high future medical costs under its self-insured medical plan due to the premature birth of the employee's infant.[17] The company argued that ERISA protects only employees who are already participating in the plan, but the court ruled that participants also include employees who *may become* eligible to receive benefits.

Thus, while you may establish reasonable classifications with respect to participation in your employee benefits plans, you would be ill-advised to single out individual employees or groups of employees for purposes of exclusion.

"Leased Employees"

Another area of confusion lies in the leased employee rules of the Internal Revenue Code—which may apply to any contingent worker supplied by a staffing firm (not solely to leased employees). Tax-qualified benefits plans, such as pension plans, may not discriminate in favor of highly compensated employees but must cover a certain percentage of non–highly compensated employees.[18] In an effort to circumvent these coverage requirements, some companies excluded non–highly compensated employees from their plans by "firing" these employees, transferring them to the payroll of leasing companies, leasing them back, and then establishing rich pension plans only for their highly compensated executives.

Section 414(n) was enacted as part of the Tax Equity and Fiscal

Responsibility Act of 1982 to address the abuses of employee leasing by including these transferred workers in applying the coverage requirements. As a result, workers who are not common law employees of the employer must be treated as employees of that employer for determining compliance with coverage requirements. Section 414(n) defines a "leased employee" as a worker who provides services to a company (1) under an agreement between the company and the leasing organization (staffing firm), (2) on a substantially full-time basis, and (3) of a type historically performed in the company by its employees.[19] Past legislative initiatives in this area that failed to become law have sought to narrow the definition of "leased employee" by replacing the historically performed criterion with the right-to-control standard—thus restricting the attribution of such workers in testing tax-qualified plans.[20]

However, a leased employee is not treated as a company's employee if he or she is covered by a safe-harbor plan offered by the leasing organization.[21] But if leased employees constitute more than 20 percent of the company's non–highly compensated workforce, the safe harbor does not apply.[22]

Treating workers as leased employees does not automatically mean that they must participate in your company's benefits plans. The number of leased employees may be so small that these employees have no adverse impact on the discrimination tests. On the other hand, if including leased employees in discrimination testing does result in disqualification for failure to meet the coverage requirements, you may lose the tax deductions for contributions to the plan, and highly compensated employees may be taxed on the value of benefits received under the plan.

Individual Rights

Like regular core employees, contingent workers have rights in the workplace and, correspondingly, you have certain obligations to these workers. Some of the individual rights under federal law that have particular relevance for contingent staffing arrangements are summarized in Figure 7-4.

Title VII

Although your legal responsibilities for contingent workers typically require an employment relationship, you may still be liable

Figure 7-4. Individual rights under federal law.

Title VII	Prohibits discrimination on the basis of race, color, religion, sex, or national origin.
ADEA	*(Age Discrimination in Employment Act)* Prohibits discrimination against an employee who is at least 40 years of age.
ADA	*(Americans with Disabilities Act)* Prohibits discrimination on the basis of disability and requires "reasonable accommodation."
FMLA	*(Family and Medical Leave Act)* Requires provision of unpaid leave of up to 12 weeks annually for family or medical reasons, maintenance of benefits during leave, and reinstatement to same or equivalent position at expiration of leave. • Primary employer (staffing firm) is responsible for satisfying FMLA. • Secondary employer (client company) is prohibited from discriminating or retaliating against employee taking FMLA.
COBRA	*(Consolidated Omnibus Budget Reconciliation Act)* Entitles terminated employees to continuation of group health plan coverage for 18 months after a qualifying event, such as termination of employment other than for gross misconduct or following a reduction in hours.
WARN	*(Worker Adjustment and Retraining Notification)* Requires giving 60-day notice to affected employees before mass layoffs or plant closings.

Note: Employees may also have rights under state laws.

under Title VII even when such a relationship is absent. In *King v. Chrysler Corporation,* the operation of Chrysler's cafeteria was outsourced to Canteen.[23] Dawn King, a cashier who worked for Canteen at the cafeteria, was subjected to obscene gestures and inappropriate touching by a Chrysler employee. She sued both Chrysler and Canteen for failing to remedy a hostile work environment. Although Chrysler claimed King lacked an employment relationship with the company, the court rejected the argument because Title VII does not specify that the employer committing the unlawful act must employ the injured individual. The court did not rely on the notion that Chrysler was a joint employer. Rather, it appeared concerned that Chrysler might have been able to insulate itself from liability by virtue of its contingent staffing relationship with Canteen.

In working with your staffing firm or outsource provider, one
course of action is to have that firm or provider put in place a procedure to respond to problems occurring in your workplace that affect
contingent workers assigned to your company. For example, developing a written policy against sexual harassment and establishing a
grievance procedure might be part of that response. Then, should a
complaint be made, concerted action by you and your staffing firm
to investigate and, if necessary, remedy the offense quickly may spare
you legal headaches later. The policy should assign the principal in-
vestigatory and decision-making responsibility to the employer of the
contingent worker—the staffing firm.

Disability Discrimination

The Americans with Disabilities Act (ADA) prohibits discrimination of the basis of disability. It imposes an affirmative duty on employers to provide reasonable accommodation to a job applicant or
employee when that disabled person is able to perform the essential
functions of the job. "Reasonable accommodation" is defined as
modifications or adjustments to the job application process, work environment, or benefits and privileges of employment. It may include
job restructuring, modified work schedules, reassignment, special
equipment, aids, or services, and accessibility to facilities.[24]
The ADA specifically prohibits an employer from participating
in a "contractual or other arrangement" that subjects an otherwise
qualified applicant or employee to disability discrimination.[25] Thus,
a job-site employer may not instruct its staffing firm to screen candidates for disabilities.
The ADA, however, does not directly address the responsibilities
of a job-site employer and staffing firm in a joint employer situation
or, more specifically, just who should bear the cost of providing reasonable accommodation. Practically speaking, the job-site employer
may be required to make reasonable accommodation for those workers, especially since that employer is in the better position to assess
any accommodation of the duties to be performed in the workplace.

Family and Medical Leave

The Family and Medical Leave Act (FMLA) requires an employer
to provide to its employees unpaid leave of 12 weeks in any 12-month

period for the birth or adoption of a child, care of a child, spouse, or parent with a serious health condition, or serious health condition of the employee. The employer must maintain health benefits for the employee on leave and must reinstate that employee following the leave to the same or an equivalent position.[26]

In a joint employment situation, both employers have obligations under the FMLA. Whether joint employment exists is determined by viewing the relationship in its totality. Once such a situation is found to exist, the FMLA delineates the responsibilities of the primary employer and secondary employer. When a staffing firm supplies workers to a client company, the primary employer is typically the staffing firm and the secondary employer is the client company.[27]

In such a situation, the staffing firm would be responsible for required notices, FMLA leave, health benefits maintenance, and job restoration. The client company would be responsible for accepting the employee returning from FMLA leave in lieu of the replacement employee as long as the staffing firm continues to supply that company with workers and wishes to place the returning employee with the same company. In addition to these responsibilities, of course, the client company has the obligations of a primary employer with respect to its core workforce.[28]

Labor Relations

Under the National Labor Relations Act (NLRA), a company may not take action against its employees, such as transferring its employees to the payroll of a staffing firm, for exercising their rights to organize.[29] Certain labor relations issues involving contingent workers, which are highlighted in this section, may arise, particularly when you use workers supplied by a staffing firm on a long-term basis.

Eligibility to Vote

Under certain circumstances, a contingent worker may be entitled to vote in a representation election. In *NLRB v. S.R.D.C., Inc.*,[30] a temporary worker participated in the representation election, resulting ultimately in the certification of the union as the exclusive bargaining agent. The temporary worker was terminated one week after the election, but had not been told in advance that he would be laid off on a certain date. In upholding the vote of the temporary worker, the court based its decision on the fact that no termination date was known and the worker was employed on the election date. Thus, as this case illustrates, a company with a significant number of contingent workers would be well-advised to set fixed termination dates for its contingent workers. Otherwise, the company may be faced with a unionized workforce determined by individuals who are no longer working there.

Liability of a Joint Employer

When you are a joint employer, you have all the obligations of an employer under the NLRA with respect to your contingent workers. The focus of the joint employer analysis is on whether two separate entities control the same group of employees. If your company and the staffing firm share or jointly determine matters governing the essential terms and conditions of employment, joint employer status exists.[31] If no joint employer relationship exists, you will most likely be immune from the economic strength of the union and cannot be bound to a collective bargaining agreement signed by your staffing firm. You are also free to "fire" the staffing firm without being held liable for unfair labor practices.[32]

However, if you are found to be a joint employer with your staffing firm whose contingent workers on your premises are engaged in organizing a union, terminating your contract with the staffing firm may be in violation of the NLRA, as was the case in *American Air Filter Company* (AAF).[33] Under its leasing contract with Transport Associates to supply drivers, AAF could reject any driver it did not like. AAF provided complete supervision of the workers, and otherwise treated them as though they were employees. Transport Associates interviewed and hired the drivers, issued weekly paychecks, and included the drivers in its benefits programs. After the truck drivers' union negotiated a new, more expensive contract with Transport, AAF terminated its leasing arrangement, as was its prerogative under the contract. Following the union's appeal to the National Labor Relations Board, the administrative law judge found in favor of the union. Since AAF had given Transport Associates the role of negotiating wages with the union, it was then bound by the terms Transport Associates had negotiated. Because of its day-to-day control over the leased employees, AAF had a mandatory duty to bargain before terminating the contract.

As a joint employer with your staffing firm, you can also be held vicariously liable for the unlawful practices of the staffing firm. Labor law has evolved two distinct standards for vicarious liability depending on the degree of your involvement in the joint employer relationship.

If you are a "traditional" joint employer, you may be held liable as well when your staffing firm engages in unlawful acts. In a traditional joint employer arrangement under the NLRA, your company and the staffing firm essentially share responsibility for every aspect of the employment relationship, including hiring, firing, discipline, supervision, and direction.[34] You are likely to be vicariously liable when the contingent staffing arrangement is of long duration and is integrated into your business operations.

By contrast, where a staffing firm's role is very limited—for example, recruiting and supplying workers and administering the payroll—you will be held liable for your staffing firm's unlawful acts only if you knew (or should have known) about the act and acquiesced by failing to protest or resist such acts.[35] Thus, if you are considered a joint employer with your staffing firm and you know that the firm has unlawfully discharged the joint employees for engaging in union activities and you do nothing, you will also be held liable. This "knowledge-plus-failure-to-act" standard of vicarious liability applies to the vast majority of contingent staffing arrangements.

Workers' Compensation

Prior to a wave of state reforms, workers' compensation was an area in which employee leasing arrangements were often used to attempt to circumvent the rules. A company with a poor experience rating could fire its workforce, transfer the employees to the payroll of a leasing firm, and lease the employees back. As a result, the company could obtain lower workers' compensation rates based on the experience modifications of the leasing firm—and could repeat the process with another leasing firm once its poor experience was reflected in the record of the first leasing firm.

In response to such fraudulent practices, several states have adopted a model regulation drafted by the National Association of Insurance Commissioners (NAIC).[36] The NAIC model regulation requires leasing firms—temporary help firms are generally exempted—to obtain operating licenses. When leased employees are covered through a standard workers' compensation policy issued to a leasing firm, the leasing firm is generally required to maintain separate policies covering the leased employees of each lessee and the exposure and experience of the lessee to be used in determining the premium for such policy.[37]

A single workers' compensation policy generally protects *both* your company and your staffing firm from suits in tort when a contingent worker suffers a workplace injury. This is one area in which you gain significant benefit by virtue of being a joint employer with your staffing firm. Your protection is derived from the employer-employee relationship you have with the contingent worker. If the employee of a staffing firm working for you is considered a "lent employee," you become a "special employer" entitled to statutory immunity from tort suits. A lent employee is one who is (1) under a contract with the special employer which is implied from the acceptance of that employer's direction and control, (2) performing work of the special employer, and (3) subject to the special employer's right to control the details of the work.

In sum, if you expect your staffing firm to provide workers' compensation for contingent workers supplied to your company, you must check the laws with respect to the following:[38]

- Ensure that your staffing firm, if an employee leasing organization, is properly registered.
- Know your liability in case a contingent worker sues you for damages in excess of the workers' compensation award. (A contractual indemnification from your staffing firm backed by liability insurance coverage may remedy this problem.)
- Check whether you will be held directly liable for payment or workers' compensation benefits even when the staffing firm has agreed to provide coverage. (A special clause in your contract may allow the staffing firm's carrier to pay benefits to you if state law prevents direct payment to the worker by the staffing firm.)

Managing Intelligently by Minimizing Your Risks

Managing a workforce that includes contingent workers requires you to be alert to the complexities of your relationships to these workers.

As this chapter illustrates, you retain some responsibilities toward your contingent workers even when they are employees of a staffing company. Thus, in order for you to successfully manage a mixed workforce of core and contingent workers, you must proceed not only with your workers in mind, but within the framework of the law.

From a legal perspective, the best action for your company is to plan carefully so as to avoid exposure to unnecessary liability. As companies have learned to their detriment, when legal problems arise, contingent workers are likely to point to the job-site employer even if they are employees of a staffing firm. Moreover, if a lawsuit or grievance is filed, these workers are likely to have the sympathy of the judge or agency hearing the case.

Eliminate Ad Hoc Staffing Practices

An important step for any company is to eliminate the existence of any ad hoc contingent staffing practices. Chances are that your company already has an "invisible workforce"—contingent workers who perhaps have attained an almost permanent status in the company. These workers were probably brought in long ago for a specific purpose in a specific department, but have then been allowed to continue working on their original assignment or on other jobs, especially if head count restrictions prevent permanent additions to the staff. When this is the case, and the workers are supplied by a staffing firm, your company would be required, at the very least, to include them as leased employees in testing tax-qualified benefit plans. However, if the workers were directly hired and meet the minimum participation requirements for tax-qualified plans, they should not be excluded from such plans.

In order to deal effectively with these situations, you need to first identify the dimensions of the problem by conducting audits in areas you consider most vulnerable to ad hoc staffing arrangements. The self-audit form shown in Figure 7-5 can help you assess the status of your contingent worker arrangements.

Clarify the Boundaries

Another way to avoid problems is to delineate clearly the boundaries of any contingent work relationship so that appearances, as well as

Figure 7-5. A contingent workforce self-audit.

All Contingent Workers Currently Working in Your Department
1. Contingent workers on your company's payroll:
   a. Total number currently at work _____
   b. Number who have worked more than 6 months _____
2. Contingent workers who are *not* company employees:
   a. Total number currently at work _____
   b. Number who have worked more than 6 months _____
3. Contingent workers who have worked more than 6 months:

	Total Number	No. Working 1,000+ Hours
On Your Company's Payroll:		
a. On-call part-timers	_____	_____
b. Direct-hire temps	_____	_____
Not Company Employees:		
c. Temps supplied by a staffing firm	_____	_____
d. Leased employees	_____	_____
e. Employees of an outsourced operation	_____	_____
f. Independent contractors/freelancers	_____	_____

Contingent Workers Who Are Not Company Employees
4. Extent of supervision by a company employee (check appropriate boxes):

	Never	Seldom	Sometimes	Frequently	Always
Temps from staffing firm	☐	☐	☐	☐	☐
Leased employees	☐	☐	☐	☐	☐
Outsourced employees	☐	☐	☐	☐	☐
Independent contractors	☐	☐	☐	☐	☐

5. Nature of supervision provided in question 4—for example, training, work projects or assignments, hours worked:
   Temps from staffing firm _____
   Leased employees _____
   Outsourced employees _____
   Independent contractors _____

worker expectations, match your company's intentions for using these workers. You should be up front with your contingent workers about the temporary nature of their work assignments and provide visible evidence of the distinctions between your core and contingent employees. (See also Chapter 2.) The following practices may help to underscore these distinctions:

- Provide managers with guidelines for using contingent workers, including time limits on assignments to prevent the proliferation of "permanent" temporaries.
- Make distinctions where possible between types of jobs to be done by core and contingent workers. Avoid using contingent workers in critical areas of the business where in-house expertise should be retained or where confidentiality is important.
- Maintain a separate payroll for your casual part-timers and direct-hire temporaries. This accounting procedure reinforces your separate treatment of these workers if they do not receive all benefits or other privileges of core employment.
- Have a staffing company representative on-site to handle human resources management issues that arise with your contingent workers. (The staffing firm representative is a surrogate supervisor and locus of temporary workers' concerns. This arrangement is not only for appearances' sake, but also improves the climate for the contingent workers and provides a channel for redress of problems before they get serious, without occupying too much of your supervisors' time.)
- Transfer contingent workers on your payroll to a staffing firm if long-term use of these workers is contemplated or desirable.
- Make sure that contracts with independent contractors identify specific projects to be completed, and make payments that coincide with delivery dates during the project period.
- Ensure that you are not the only client for your independent contractors by asking them to furnish evidence of their independent business operation. Avoid the appearance of an employer-employee relationship by not using their services full-time for long periods, and by not providing job titles, dedicated office space, or dedicated support staff.
- Provide ID cards for contingent workers that differentiate them from your core workforce.

- Avoid giving perks, such as access to the company store or invitations to the company picnic, to your contingent workers.

In implementing safeguards, you need to weigh the advantages of distinguishing your contingent workers from your core employees against the potential disadvantages of creating or exacerbating a two-tier workforce. As previous chapters have shown, companies need to find solutions that will work for them in their own corporate environment. In any case, however, your counsel should be consulted in implementing and maintaining prudent contingent staffing arrangements.

Endnotes

1. *Hill v. Eastman Kodak Co.*, No. 94-CV-6353T (W.D.N.Y.); *Penix v. Eastman Kodak Co.*, No. 94-CV-6352T (W.D.N.Y.).
2. Michael P. Cronin, "Does This Look Like an Employee to You?" *Inc.,* September 1994, p. 50.
3. Commission of the Future of Worker-Management Relations, *Report and Recommendations,* 1994, pp. 35–41.
4. IRC § 3509.
5. Coopers & Lybrand, *Projection of the Loss in Federal Tax Revenues Due to Misclassification of Workers,* June 1994. The IRS has estimated that one employer in seven misclassifies its workers, and approximately three million employees are misclassified as independent contractors. "IRS Inquiry: Is Worker at IBM Really a Contractor?" *The New York Times,* July 6, 1995, p. D3.
6. Jaclyn Fierman, "The Contingency Work Force," *Fortune,* January 24, 1994, pp. 30, 34. *See also* Barbara Ettore, "The Contingency Workforce Moves Mainstream," *Management Review,* February 1994, p. 15.
7. S. 2357, 103d Cong., 2d Sess. (1994). Further, Congress has shown interest in removing the uncertainty of who is an employee versus an independent contractor by introducing legislation to clarify the distinction. *See, e.g.,* H.R. 1972, 104th Cong., 1st Sess. (1995); H.R. 582, 104th Cong., 1st Sess. (1995).
8. Revenue Act of 1978, § 530(a), Pub. L. No. 95-600, 92 Stat. 2885 (1978). There is some debate as to whether a company must concede that its workers are common law employees before Section 530 relief is available. *See* Guy Vander Jagt *et al.*, "The Significance of the IRS Shift on Worker Classification," *Tax Notes,* June 19, 1995, p. 1677; "IRS Reverses Field on Worker Classification," *Tax Notes,* June 5, 1995, p. 1381.

9. Cronin, p. 57.
10. Tax Reform Act of 1986, § 1706, Pub. L. No. 99-514, 100 Stat. 2871 (1986). The reason for the technical service worker exception was Congress's concern that Section 530 created competitive unfairness in rewarding companies that aggressively took the position that their workers were independent contractors and thereby resulting in substantial noncompliance with respect to employment tax issues. The enactment of the exception was apparently the result of successful lobbying by large technical service firms. It was estimated in 1991 that the exception affected 80,000 technical service workers. Staff of Joint Comm. on Taxation, *General Explanation of the Tax Reform Act of 1986*, 100th Cong., 1st Sess. 1343–44 (1987). Dan R. Mastromarco, "The Rekindling Independent Contractor Debate," *Tax Notes*, November 4, 1991, p. 603.
11. No. 89-CV73046-DT, 1990 WL 259676 (E.D. Mich. December 20, 1990).
12. On the other hand, a company may be liable for FICA and income taxes if it lends funds to a staffing firm for the purpose of paying wages to employees the staffing firm supplies to work for that company, and it has knowledge (or ought to have knowledge) that the employer does not intend to withhold and remit these taxes. The company's liability would be limited to 25 percent of the value of the funds provided to the employer. IRC § 3505(b).
13. 3 F.3d 1488 (11th Cir. 1993).
14. Section 510 of ERISA provides: "It shall be unlawful for any person to discharge, fine, suspend, expel, discipline, or discriminate against a participant . . . for the purpose of interfering with the attainment of any right to which such participant may become entitled under the [employee benefit] plan [or Title I of ERISA]. . . ." ERISA § 510, 29 U.S.C. § 1140.
15. *See* IRC § 410(a).
16. 966 F.2d 1104 (7th Cir. 1992).
17. 948 F.2d 993 (6th Cir. 1991).
18. IRC § 410(b).
19. IRC § 414(n). "Substantially full-time basis" means that during any consecutive 12-month period, the worker has performed services for the recipient (company) for at least 1,500 hours or, alternatively, a number of hours of service at least equal to 75 percent of the average number of hours customarily performed by an employee of that recipient in the particular position. IRS Notice 84-11, 1982-2 C.B. 469, Q&A-7; *see also* IRS Worksheet (Form 8386) & Explanation No. 8, Employee Leasing.
20. *E.g.*, S. 1732, 102d Cong., 1st Sess. (1991).
21. A plan is considered safe harbor if it meets the following requirements: (1) the leasing organization contributions to a nonintegrated money purchase pension plan of at least 10 percent of each leased employee's com-

pensation; (2) the plan covers all employees of the leasing organization; and (3) the plan provides for full and immediate vesting. IRC § 414(n) (5) (B).

22. IRC § 414(n) (5) (A) (ii).
23. 812 F. Supp. 151 (E.D. Mo. 1993). However, a recent decision by a New York state court found that a temporary worker assigned by a temp agency to a bank was the employee of the agency and not the bank. *Bowles v. State Div. of Human Rts.,* No. 404783/94 (N.Y. Sup. Ct., April 20, 1995).
24. 29 U.S.C. § 12111 *et seq.* A defense to providing reasonable accommodation is "undue hardship"—any accommodation that would be unduly costly, extensive, substantial, or disruptive, or would fundamentally alter the nature or operation of the business. *Id.* §§ 12111 (10) (A), 12112 (b) (5) (A).
25. *Id.* § 12112 (b) (2).
26. 29 U.S.C. § 2601 *et seq.* Eligible employees from FMLA leave must have been employed for at least 12 months prior to taking a leave, and must have worked at least 1,250 hours during that 12-month period.
27. The primary employer is the entity with authority or responsibility to hire and fire, assign or place the employee, make payroll, and provide employment benefits. 29 C.F.R. § 825.106(c).
28. *Id.* § 825.106(e).
29. *MPC Plating Inc. v. NLRB,* 912 F.2d 883 (6th Cir. 1990).
30. 45 F.3d 328 (9th Cir. 1995).
31. *See, e.g., NLRB v. Western Temporary Services, Inc.,* 821 F.2d 1258, 1266 (7th Cir. 1987).
32. *Clinton's Ditch Co-op., Inc. v. NLRB,* 778 F.2d 132 (2d Cir. 1985), *cert. denied,* 479 U.S. 814 (1986).
33. 258 N.L.R.B. 49 (1981).
34. *Capitol EMI Music, Inc.,* 311 N.L.R.B., 997 (1993), *aff'd,* 23 F.3d 399 (4th Cir. 1994).
35. *Id.; America's Best Quality Coatings Corp.,* 313 N.L.R.B. No. 470 (1993), *aff'd,* 44 F.3d 516 (7th Cir.), *cert. denied,* 115 S. Ct. 2609 (1995).
36. Louise Kertesz, "Employee Leasing Firms Can Cut Some Benefit Costs; But Bad Apples Means Buyer Beware," *Business Insurance,* March 29, 1993, p. 10.
37. National Association of Insurance Commissioners Employee Leasing Model Regulation.
38. Edward A. Lenz, *Co-Employment: Employer Liability Issues in Staffing Services Arrangements* (Second Edition), National Association of Temporary and Staffing Services, 1994.

8
Summing Up and Looking Ahead

The contingent workforce, as a pair of words, came into the lexicon in the mid-1980s. The contingent workforce, as a group of people doing jobs, has been around for a long, long time. We have always had part-time employees and temporaries from agencies. But the contingent workforce of today means something quite different from the part-timers and temps of yesterday. The contingent workforce now is on the front pages of the daily business press. It is important to companies, and it is a topic of managerial conversation. Contingent work is at the center of the radically changing relationship between companies and workers. Contingent workers are peripheral workers, but contingent work is an integral part of business strategy.

The driver is flexibility. Companies need flexibility to adjust quickly the amount of labor they use, now more than ever before. Contingent labor provides that flexibility. Here today, gone tomorrow. But like all good things, contingent labor is a mixed blessing. Contrary to the usual assumption, contingent workers sometimes are not a cost-effective solution to the flexibility problem. They do not simplify managers' jobs as much as it seems, but instead pose some new management issues of their own. And there are equity issues in the background. To be a good manager of contingent workers—to gain the pluses and miss the minuses—requires sober reflection and intelligent decision making.

In this chapter we look across the issues and information of the previous seven chapters, and we take a look ahead to the future of the contingent workforce in companies. We begin with the recent growth in numbers and the changing roles for contingent workers in the business strategy of companies. We go on to synthesize the management issues that must be addressed.

The New Concept of Contingent Labor

The term *contingent workforce* is imprecise, so we need to stress exactly what it is. Contingent workers are people with little or no attachment to the company at whose place of business they work. When and how much they work depends on the company's call. Their work schedule is irregular. They have no job security and no implicit contract for continued employment. These are essential defining conditions. In practice, contingent workers are temporaries from staffing companies (also called agencies or help supply services), and they are hourly part-time employees (but note that some part-time employees are regular employees and not contingent). Contingent workers are also direct-hire or in-house temporaries, workers from leasing companies, and independent short-term contractors.

Growth in Numbers

What first attracts attention to the contingent workforce is its apparent rapid growth. That is only a half-truth. Yes, the rate of use of temporaries from staffing companies has been growing very fast, boosted in part by the strongly growing economy since 1983 (except for the short and mild recession between 1990 and 1991). But they are the smallest component of the contingent workforce. And yes, employment in the business services industry has been growing very fast. But only a fraction of these employees are contingent workers, and they are a small share of the total contingent workforce. In contrast, part-time employment has not increased as a share of the total workforce in more than 25 years (although there was a sizable uptick in involuntary part-time employment in 1991 caused by the recession). Growth in self-employment, which includes independent short-term contractors, has recently leveled off.

No one knows exactly how many contingent workers there are because no one has counted them according to a subjective definition like that above (this gap is being filled with new data from the U.S. Bureau of Labor Statistics). In the meantime, the estimate in this book is that contingent workers accounted for 20 to 25 percent of all U.S. employment in 1993. That is a big number even if it is not a fast-growing number.

Changes in Roles and Relationships

What is new about the contingent workforce, beyond the growth in its numbers, is something much deeper: roles and relationships. Roles means the types of functions and tasks that contingent workers carry out. Relationships refers to the tacit linkages between companies and workers. Both the roles of contingent workers and the relationships of workers to companies are undergoing fundamental change.

Contingent work has gone beyond the traditional stereotypical fill-in, peak-load assignments of secretary and bank teller. Now we also see interim company presidents who are contingent workers. Lawyers and computer programmers are contingent. We see large numbers of jobs in manufacturing plants staffed by contingent workers. Contingent work is now a central way for companies to get their work done. It is how they achieve the very important objective of flexibility. Contingent work is an integral part of business strategy. It is in the mainstream. It is a way of thinking. What is new and different is how and where contingent workers are used.

The case should not be overstated, however. Temporary and part-time workers continue to do their traditional jobs, and they are still concentrated in low-skill and low-wage occupations and industries. Nationwide, they are overrepresented in clerical, sales, and service jobs. Within work units inside companies, we see a similar pattern: many contingent workers bunched in one or two low-end job grades. But the distribution is bimodal. There are also sizable numbers of part-timers, temporaries, or independent contractors in high-end technical and professional jobs.

The rise of the contingent workforce is aided and abetted by the changing corporate ethos. The continuing trends toward downsizing, restructuring, and reengineering complement and stimulate contingent labor. Outsourcing now goes beyond the buying-in of manufactured components; it includes the farming out of entire business functions including human resources management itself. Employment security is a thing of the past—hardly any U.S. company mentions it anymore; even the term *permanent* employee is banished in favor of *regular* employee. Corporate-sponsored career management is treated carefully (that would imply a future set of jobs in the company). "Employability" is now the individual's responsibility. All this fits very nicely with the concept of contingent labor. If the old psychological contract between company and employee is broken, contingent labor is in the breach.

What is new about contingent labor is not only that it is a growing part of the workforce, but also that it is an increasingly central feature of business strategy rather than a peripheral practice.

The Equity Concern

Along with the growth in numbers of contingent workers and the increasingly important role they play in companies, we see a corresponding growth in concern about how contingent workers fare in the workplace as individuals compared to regular employees. We also see concern about the long-term implications for business and society of permanently expanded use of contingent workers on the prevailing current terms.

Data on who contingent workers are and how they are rewarded give rise to this concern. Contingent workers tend to be younger than regular employees, and they are more likely to be women. They have only a little less education, but probably quite a lot less human capital after considering their presumed smaller amount of training and experience. (Keep in mind that this overall gross picture conceals vast differences within the ranks of contingent workers, especially among independent contractors about whom we have no statistical data.)

Contingent workers are paid less than regular employees on the average. Much of the overall wage gap simply reflects the gap in occupations that separate contingent from regular employees, and differences in their organizational tenure. Nevertheless, there are plenty of instances of contingent workers who do the same job as regular employees in the same company, but are paid less. (In contrast to this average picture, some specialized professionals who are contingent workers are paid premium wages.) If contingent workers are paid less, perhaps this wage inequality comes from their typically younger age and shorter length of service with the company where they work. That is a rational explanation of the fact, but the fact of wage inequality remains.

Very few contingent workers get any benefits. Expensive benefits that have value only in the distant future and are hard to prorate to time worked, like pension plans, are not expected to be received by contingent workers. But other benefits are only marginally more received. In addition, contingent workers do not get the kind of general training and skill building that comes from attachment to an employer.

In sum, and as a generalization, contingent workers have fewer resources than regular employees, and they have fewer choices. Our estimate, based on national statistics and some managers' experiences, is that about half at most of all contingent workers freely choose this status and prefer it to regular employment, at least at the time. For these people, the availability of short-term assignments allows them to get some income and experience while they pursue another important interest—such as finishing a college education, running their own business, or caring for a family. For other people who choose contingent status, the availability of contingent employment allows them to escape the implicit obligations of regular employment, ranging from overtime work to changing jobs and locations when the company asks.

The other half or more of the contingent workforce has no other alternative, or at best uses contingent work instrumentally to get into (or back into) the regular workforce. If these people begin with fewer resources and get less from contingent employment than they would from regular employment, then we encounter the long-term concern about worsening the division in the labor force between the more well-off and the less well-off. This is a concern to society of course, but it is also a concern to companies that depend on a future workforce of capable people.

Perspectives on the Growth of Contingent Labor: Will It Continue?

The growth in the numbers of contingent workers and the transformation of contingent labor into an integral component of business strategy are driven by a set of microlevel business needs and a set of macrolevel forces. They can all be reduced to these words: change, flexibility, and costs.

Companies want to use contingent workers for one or more of four reasons. First, some companies need the flexibility to closely match the size of the workforce to the amount of work to be done, and they need to quickly change the former to track the latter. They also need flexibility to acquire specialized expertise on an as-needed basis. Second, some companies want to buffer their regular workforce against the shocks of boom and bust in the business cycle, or they want to protect their regular workforce from the redeployments that need to occur as products and markets change. Third, some companies believe that contingent workers are cheaper than regular workers because their pay and benefits can be less. They also believe that controlling head count contains costs, and contingent workers are not part of head counts. Fourth, some companies want to ease management tasks and cut personnel overhead. In each of these four cases, managers see contingent labor as a potential solution. Of course, traditional reasons for using contingent workers still apply, such as filling in for absent employees and screening candidates for future employment.

Outside the domain of any one manager or company, strong forces push the use of contingent labor. Turbulent global markets force the pace of change and impose cost pressure. Service industries and jobs expand. Downsizing and restructuring continue without letup. These forces raise the overall demand for contingent labor, which promises the flexibility to cope with change at reasonable cost.

If demand is strong, is supply ample? On the one hand, it is clear that in the supply of people who are contingent workers, many would rather be regular employees. But that supply so far has been ample. Even though contingent worker wages are lower and unemployment rates higher than for regular employees, the supply is quite adequate. Even when unemployment rates overall go fairly low, contingent labor still has been available. Managers' experiences confirm this. So the usage of contingent labor could go on increasing.

Will it continue? Will the macro forces and micro needs that drive contingent labor stay with us? No one will predict that globalization of markets will stop; that process has a long way to go, especially with the advent of many transition economies. Service industry growth might abate but not cease. Downsizing and restructuring, once thought to be recession phenomena, now are predicted by business managers themselves to go on throughout the rest of the 1990s. The externally driven demand for contingent labor looks to be strong well into the future.

Next, look inside companies. Does anyone predict that company needs for flexibility will shrink? Will workload fluctuations diminish?

Will business cycles flatten out? Will new product and new market redeployments slow down? Will cost pressures get less severe? While scientific prognostications are not at hand, we guess a majority of managers would say no to these questions. The internal need for contingent labor will also apparently remain strong.

Two critical questions about the future growth of contingent labor remain. First, will the supply of people who are willing to work contingently stay ample? If not, their price will go up or their quality will go down, and either would reduce their usage. Second, can companies manage contingent labor so that it meets their flexibility needs cost-effectively for the company and equitably for the workers? Putting aside the labor supply prediction, we turn next to the issues about managing contingent workers.

Issues in Managing Contingent Workers

Managers need to know how to structure and manage a contingent workforce so that it delivers on its potential. The main objective of flexibility is easily achieved with contingent workers. Whether it's coping with day-to-day fluctuations in workload or long swings of the business cycle, contingent labor works. However, the objective of cutting labor cost might not be achieved, our experience tells us. And the objective of easing management tasks is achieved only at management's peril. What can be done to make these dubious achievements more certain?

Recommended management practices are not always in sync with advice from legal counsel. Whereas equitable and compassionate treatment of employees is at the heart of good management practice, your legal advisors are likely to urge a much more cautious—and distant—relationship with contingent workers. Both sides of this argument are set forth in this book. In the end, you must weigh these alternatives in light of your company's values and culture, and choose a course of action that works best in your particular situation.

Productivity and Performance

The evidence is only anecdotal, but the theory is clear. Contingent workers are probably going to be a little less productive than regular employees. On both skill and effort, contingent workers are likely to fall a little short. In terms of averages (leaving aside the high-end professionals), contingent workers typically have less education, training, and experience, and will always have less time on the current job than regular employees. They will sometimes have less motivation to work hard (with one important exception discussed later in this section). In our experience, managers easily say that contingent and regular workers are "about the same" in productivity; factual checks show they are not.

All this refers to individual productivity. Sometimes what really counts is work unit performance. That comes from teamwork. This is a second strike against contingent workers. No matter how good they are as individual workers, they cannot be really effective team members if they don't stay with the team for a while, and contingent workers cannot stay for a long enough while. This means that high-performance contingent labor is restricted to work settings that don't depend heavily on teamwork.

Raising the productivity and performance of contingent workers is like traversing a slippery slope. You can try to get better people—people with better skills and work habits—by improved recruiting (this is easier when the labor market is slack), by using staffing companies that can find the people you need better than you can, or by providing more and better training. The problem is that these options cost money. Will you come out ahead, or will you stumble on that slick incline?

You can try to get more effort from contingent workers, given their skill. Work effort comes from motivation. Motivation has many sources, including involvement, security, and fair rewards. Involvement and security are ruled out by definition for contingent workers. Neither commitment nor loyalty to the company can be expected if it is not reciprocated. Your scope for action is limited. What you can do is to pay for performance—give merit pay for contingent workers so that higher performers get higher pay. If output is easily measurable, performance is easily determined. But if it is not, then you have to do performance appraisals. That adds a management step, and it takes a step toward making you a co-employer of your contingent workers if they are supplied by a staffing company. At the very least, you can provide equitable wages and benefits.

There is an important opposite case. If contingent workers want to change to regular employment and the company where they work recruits new regular employees from its contingent workforce, then a strong motivator to do good work is present. Another way to raise the productivity of contingent workers, then, is to use the contingent workforce as an entry port into regular employment.

For some companies, the issue of the productivity of contingent workers appears to be beside the point. In some jobs, output depends mostly on technology and machinery, and not much on worker skill or effort. In some jobs that are either repetitive or stressful, short-term interrupted working, as it comes from contingent workers, is best. So the productivity of contingent workers depends on the types of jobs they are asked to do.

Cost-Effectiveness

This is the blind spot of contingent labor. It is usually assumed, but seldom checked out. Contingent labor can and does cut labor costs for many companies. Less pay (or even equal pay) with no benefits and less personnel overhead compared to regular employees adds up to lots of dollars. But cost-effectiveness also depends on productivity, which we claim is usually less (and illustrate quantitatively in two of our case studies).

The comparison cannot stop there. Employment costs in addition to wages are likely to be incurred that are fixed per person and spent up-front. The most notable example is training. Usually some training is required at company expense even for contingent workers. Whether or not employment costs such as training are repaid to the company depends on how long the workers on whose behalf the costs were incurred stay on the job, or with the company. Contingent workers do not stay long. Either they go of their own volition, or the company limits their length of service. If they leave before their training costs have been recovered by the company, it is as if their wages were higher than they actually are. In our three case studies, contingent labor was actually more costly than regular employment in one company, probably more costly in another, and cheaper in the third.

What to do? Perhaps higher-cost contingent labor is simply the price to be paid for flexibility. Perhaps contingent labor is still better than overtime and layoffs. Your company's objectives and its culture will tell you whether these answers are usable in your situations.

Alternatively, we can try to improve the cost-effectiveness of contingent labor. Look at the first two ingredients: wages and benefits.

There is not much scope for reduction here—benefits are already zero in most cases, and wages are already low; reductions might lead to too few people willing to work contingently. Or an attempt could be made to raise productivity, but this is hard to do for contingent workers, as described earlier.

Next, attack the fixed up-front training costs themselves, in any one of four ways: (1) Hire already fully trained people if they can be found—but then expect to pay higher wages. (2) Shift training to staffing companies by using temporaries from them who meet your specifications, and pay a fee to them; this could be cheaper than hiring contingent workers yourself and training them. (3) Simplify the jobs so that less training is required; let machines do the training-intensive part—except that overly simple jobs have limitations of their own. (4) Or pay an initially lower "training wage" to new contingent workers during their training period, and then increase their wage when they are fully productive. This scheme marries two good concepts: cost sharing of training between company and worker, and pay for performance.

Finally, improve the chances of recovering your up-front training costs, whatever they are, by extending the time on the job of trained contingent workers. Get them to stay longer by raising their wages for longer service, tailoring a package of benefits to their special needs, giving them a specified certain-duration short-term contract, or hiring them into the regular workforce after a certain length of time. These are all good ideas, and they are all practiced by some companies.

However, they expose a fundamental dilemma in achieving cost-effective contingent labor. Long-service and contingent work are a contradiction. Contingent work by definition is short-term. To get contingent workers to stay on the job long enough to be cost-effective will be both quite difficult and risky. It will be difficult because the workers have other major interests that will take them away from you. It will be risky because long-serving workers are likely to be regarded by themselves and others as employees whether you want that or not. "Permanent" temporaries are a bad idea.

If the cost-effectiveness of contingent labor cannot be improved, the remaining decision for managers to make is to use fewer of them. We know from company experience that many times more contingent workers are used than are needed to achieve the company's flexibility objective; some can be terminated. In some cases, it might be possible to smooth out workload fluctuations to reduce the need for flexibility. Or in the spirit of reengineering, maybe some flexibility needs can be minimized.

How Do Contingent Workers Fit With Core Employees?

If your reason for using contingent workers is to achieve flexibility, as is true for most companies, the chances are that you want to have both contingent workers and regular core employees at the same facility. Then you encounter three related questions about how to manage a mixed core-contingent workforce:

1. How many contingent workers should you use?
2. What work should contingent workers do, and are these the same jobs or different jobs from those done by core employees?
3. How much movement from contingent to core employment can take place, if any?

Number of Contingent Workers to Employ

The facile but apt answer to the question of how many contingent workers to use is as many as you need, but not more. Accomplish your flexibility objective and stop with that. (See Chapter 2 for a checklist of factors to help determine the number to use.) Think in terms of limiting and minimizing the size of your contingent workforce.

We offer this suggestion for two reasons. First, we have doubts that contingent workers are generally much cheaper or easier to manage than core employees. If they are cheaper because they are paid less and get no benefits, training, or other management services, then you are gambling on potential long-term damage to the workforce in return for short-term gain—not a course of action to take lightly. Second, we believe that the number of contingent workers used tends quite naturally in corporations to become too big over time unless it is watched. The numbers grow because of downsizing that is overdone or done crudely, because of the rule of head count that makes it easier to spend money on external resources including labor than to employ people internally, and because of the lack of clear strategies for contingent staffing that allows invisible creep in their numbers over time.

Types of Jobs for Contingent Workers

The type of work for which contingent workers are best suited depends on several factors. Generally, contingent workers are best suited for jobs in which (1) workload fluctuations are large, (2) initial training needs are small, (3) proprietary or core competency knowledge is not involved, and (4) independent or autonomous work rather than teamwork is practiced. In addition, (5) an ample supply of people with suitable skills must be available in the local labor market.

If the main reason to use contingent labor is to gain the flexibility to cope with fluctuating workloads, then deciding what jobs contingent workers do is easy: They do the jobs that have the biggest fluctuations in workload, as long as the training, proprietary knowledge, teamwork, and labor supply criteria permit. In this case, contingent workers and core employees are likely to do some of the same jobs some of the time.

But if the main reason to use contingent workers is to gain the flexibility to cope with long swings in the business cycle and buffer core employees from job loss, or to cut labor costs or ease management tasks, then it is not so clear what work they should do. In these cases, all the factors listed above come into play. In addition, a companion question arises: Should core and contingent workers do the same jobs?

In general, if contingent and core workers are treated differently, they probably should not do the same jobs. "Treated differently" means that their terms and conditions of employment are different—contingent workers are compensated differently, or they do not receive the same human resources management services, workplace supervision, or company perquisites. (One exception would occur when the contingent workers' jobs are of a very short-term or emergency nature. In other instances, total job segregation may not be necessary since the work could be limited to a particular aspect of a job held by a regular employee.) When they are treated differently, contingent and core workers need to constitute separate workforces. To make this succeed, your contingent workers either need to be externalized—as independent contractors or employees of a staffing company—or kept on a separate payroll.

Movement From Contingent to Core Employment

Movement of contingent workers into core employment is a natural progression, particularly if they are employees on your payroll. Managers want to hire the best people they can, and observation of people in actual working conditions is the best recruiting and screening tool. There is no reason to resist such ring-to-core movement if the contingent employees are no different in their status with the company except for the on-call nature of their work. (An analogous case is that of regular—not contingent—part-time employees whose only difference from full-time is the number of hours they work.)

However, some contingent workers should not have that mobility option. For example, if your retirees are part of your contingent workforce, your company's pension policy is likely to prohibit retirees from being employees while collecting benefits. If your contingent workers are supplied by staffing companies or are independent contractors, it is likely that you have intended to distance yourself from these workers, and separation is better, legally. In addition, their movement into the core will probably meet with resistance. Separation is better for morale among core employees. Even in these situations, however, good candidates for regular jobs can be found.

In the end, ring-to-core mobility may depend more on company strategy and corporate culture than on the legal aspects of your contingent staffing arrangements.

New Relationships With Staffing Companies

The very rapid growth in the number of temporary workers is mirrored by the growth of staffing companies that supply them. Staffing companies provide an increasing variety of staffing services to client companies and an increasing range of personnel services to their own employees. Some of these providers who supply workers on long-term leasing arrangements have extensive human resources management services for their employees. Managers who use contingent workers have to decide if these workers could best be supplied by a staffing company rather than hired directly as employees or brought in as independent contractors.

If you want to avoid having an employment relationship with your contingent workers in order to avoid certain employment taxes and benefits and certain labor relations and individual rights issues, then the use of a staffing company is potentially attractive. Caution: Note well the points made in Chapter 7—getting contingent workers from a staffing company does not mean that you have no employment relationship with your contingent workers and does not absolve you of certain management obligations. Remember also that sometimes the nature of the work to be done dictates that the contingent workers not be agency temps—for example, if substantial initial training or company-specific knowledge is needed.

Aside from allowing you to keep some distance from the thicket of legal issues, you might be able to establish relationships with staffing companies that both foster the professionalism of your contingent workforce and ease your daily supervisory tasks. To the extent that you develop a closer relationship with a staffing company, you are able to establish a more distant relationship with your contingent workers. In such a relationship, the staffing company finds the type of worker you need, trains the workers to your specifications, places a coordinator-supervisor on your premises, and pays fair wages and benefits according to your standards. In return, you give substantial long-term business to the staffing company, and, yes, you will probably pay a substantial fee. This is not necessarily a low-cost way to go. And it may be more attractive to large than small client companies, although cultivating long-term relationships with staffing companies is likely to provide benefits for them as well. For companies for whom it is possible, it is a partnership, or strategic alliance, that lets you accomplish your flexibility objective equitably.

The Way Ahead

The contingent workforce is here to stay. It does what it is supposed to do: It accomplishes its main purpose of giving companies flexibility. Temporaries, part-timers, and independent contractors are an integral part of business strategy.

Growth in the number of contingent workers will continue. Both the forces outside companies and the needs of companies themselves predict that. But the growth will be moderate, and the potential size of the contingent workforce in the future is limited.

In the future, the frequently mentioned goals we now encounter of using contingent workers to cut labor costs and ease management tasks will largely have to be abandoned. Neither is a sure bet. Flexibility is the right goal. As Tom Pierson of Hewlett-Packard said to the authors, for companies that focus on customers, hitting a multibil-lion-dollar product window is far more important than squeezing out decimal point payroll and benefit savings.

Our assessments, which are more sober than many, are based on a belief that contingent working is a flawed employment practice in need of some repairs. Contingent labor sometimes is not cost-effec-tive. Managing contingent workers is not as easy as it seems.

Cost-effectiveness is problematic partly because contingent workers are short-service; and if they are long-service they are not contingent workers. Ease of management is problematic because it is difficult to avoid some aspects of an employment relationship with contingent workers even if they are not your employees.

Equity issues accompany the use of large numbers of contingent workers. Those issues, now being questioned in public debate, will eventually have to be addressed. If contingent workers who have fewer resources and more restricted choices than regular employees also get smaller wages, no benefits, and no management services, public policy interventions are invited.

What can concerned managers do? Use contingent workers to meet a flexibility need, but do not overuse them. Know why you have contingent workers and how many you have. Do not tolerate permanent temporaries. Use large numbers of contingent workers if you need to, but only as an outcome of a strategic management deci-sion to do so. Manage core and contingent workers equitably. Allow movement from ring to core when it makes sense for your business. And do not overlook the core workforce itself as a source of an extra margin of flexibility.

In the longer term, if core workers themselves continue to lose ground in employment security and benefits, the distinctions that now separate core and contingent workers will diminish. If this is indeed the trend of the future, companies will need to find new solu-tions for managing all of their workers in ways that will provide equi-table flexibility for everyone.

Index